Mastering the PMP Exam

A Guide for Busy Professionals

Ashton Ball

Table of Contents

Introduction

Interested in learning about the unique qualities that make program managers successful? Starting from the first step, this guide will assist you in mastering the fundamental principles of program management. It's difficult for busy professionals, mid-level managers, and aspiring project managers to juggle work and preparing for the PMP exam. This book is specifically made for busy individuals like yourself who want a compact study guide.

Our study guide simplifies complex concepts, helping you become a successful program manager and ace the PMP exam. This book is invaluable whether you want to advance your career, improve project management skills, or gain foundational knowledge in a new role. Our goal is to simplify the complex world of program management for anyone dedicated to success.

Many professionals find themselves overwhelmed by the sheer volume of information they need to master for the PMP exam. Adding another responsibility to a busy day can be discouraging. Our guide considers your busy life while addressing these concerns. Each chapter is concise, focusing on the core principles and terminology you need to know without bombarding you with extraneous details. This approach allows you to absorb vital information, ensuring that every minute you invest in studying pays off.

What makes this guide unique is its focus on essential concepts over test preparation techniques. While traditional study materials often rank shortcuts and exam tricks, we believe in building a robust understanding of program management's fundamental aspects. By concentrating on the core ideas, you'll not only be prepared for the PMP exam but also equipped knowing that will serve you well throughout your career. You'll gain insights that extend beyond passing a test, laying the groundwork for real-world success in program management.

Imagine walking into the PMP exam room with confidence, knowing you've mastered the key concepts necessary for success. Picture yourself applying these principles in your daily work, leading projects more effectively, and advancing in your career with newfound expertise. This book aims to turn those visions into reality. No longer will program management seem like an insurmountable mountain; instead, it will become a series of achievable steps, each building on the last, guided by simple explanations and practical examples.

We recognize the obstacles you face and the commitment required to overcome them. Yet, with determination and the right guidance, passing the PMP exam and excelling in program management is within your reach. It might not always be easy, but it's possible. Our goal is to make the process smooth and straightforward, providing you with the tools and strategies you need to succeed.

As you embark on this journey, remember that you're not doing it alone. This book supports you through every step, breaking down complex topics into manageable sections. Each chapter aims to build your confidence and knowledge, helping you see the connections between different aspects of program management. By the end of this guide, you'll have the tools to tackle any challenge that comes your way, whether it's on the exam or in your professional life.

It's important to stay motivated and keep your end goals in sight. The path to PMP certification and becoming an outstanding program manager requires dedication, patience, and persistence. You've already taken the crucial first step by seeking this guide. Now, let's continue moving forward together. Embrace the learning process, apply what you read to real-life scenarios, and revisit sections that need more clarity. Success is a journey, not a destination. Each effort counts.

With resources and determination, you can achieve your goals. This guide is your roadmap—a trusted companion that will lead you through the intricacies of program management and help you emerge victorious on the other side. Let's dive into the essential concepts, break down the barriers to your success, and set you on a path toward becoming a certified PMP and an exceptional program manager.

So here's to your success: to mastering program management, to passing the PMP exam, and to advancing your career. Let's embark on this journey together, one essential concept at a time.

Chapter 1 - Introduction to Project Management

Project management is a key skill that enables professionals to achieve specific goals within defined constraints. It involves planning, organizing, and managing resources to bring about successful project completion. Understanding the fundamental principles of project management will set a firm foundation for anyone preparing for the Project Management Professional (PMP) exam or looking to enhance their career skills.

In this chapter, we'll explore what defines a project, differentiating it from ongoing operations through its temporary nature, specific objectives, and stakeholder involvement. We will delve into the essential aspects of projects, including timeframes, goals, and constraints, like budget and scope. We will cover the roles stakeholders play and prizing their management. Understanding these core components will equip readers to navigate the various stages of a project's lifecycle, from initiation to closure, more successful.

Definition of a Project

Projects are distinct from ongoing operations in several key ways, and understanding these differences is crucial for effective project management. We define a project as a temporary try to create a unique product, service, or result. The characteristics that distinguish projects from continuous operations include their time-bound nature, specific objectives and constraints, involvement of stakeholders, and the necessity for closure upon achieving the objectives.

Foremost, a project is temporary. This means it has a defined start and end date. Unlike regular business operations that continue indefinitely, projects have a specific purpose and accomplish particular goals. Once the project achieves those goals, they conclude it. For instance, constructing a new bridge, developing a new piece of software, or conducting a market research study are all examples of projects. Initiatives start and end with work and deliverables accomplished.

The impermanent nature of projects leads to its second characteristic: specific objectives. People undertake projects with a rational purpose in mind, whether it's creating a new product, improve a service, or achieve the specified result. The project team must define these objectives at the outset because they guide the planning and execution phases of the project. For instance, a company might launch a project to develop a new mobile app with the goal of meeting usability standards and incorporating user-requested features.

Accompanying these objectives are constraints—encompassing time, cost, and scope. Known as the project management triangle, these constraints often need careful balancing. Time determines both the length of the project and its completion deadline. The project's assigned budget determines the cost of completion. The scope outlines the specific tasks and things that need to be done to meet the project's goals. To develop our hypothetical mobile app, the team must manage the timeline, budget, and promised features and functionalities.

Stakeholders play a critical role in projects. Stakeholders can include anyone affected by the project's outcome, such as customers, team members, investors, or regulatory bodies. Successfully managing stakeholders involves identifying all people involved, understanding what they want and expect, and regularly updating them on project progress. During the construction of a new office building, stakeholders may include the construction company, business owners, employees, local government entities, and neighboring businesses or residents. Keeping these stakeholders informed and engaged is vital for the project's success.

Projects also exhibit considerable diversity in terms of size, scope, and complexity. They can range from small, straightforward tasks like organizing a company event to large-scale endeavors such as launching a nationwide marketing campaign or developing a new technology platform. Different industries also approach projects based on their specific needs and standards. For example, IT projects may involve agile methodologies with frequent iterations and feedback loops, while construction projects adhere to strict sequential phases from design to build.

The variability in project size and complexity further emphasizes the need for adaptability in project management techniques. A small project might must minimal formal documentation and a more flexible approach, because a large infrastructure project will probably need extensive planning, rigorous adherence to regulations, and detailed reporting. Industry-specific tools and software can enhance the efficiency and effectiveness of managing these projects. In the tech industry, agile tools like JIRA help teams track progress, manage backlogs, and keep high levels of communication. In contrast, construction projects might rely on specialized software for architectural design, scheduling, and resource management.

One of the most defining aspects of a project is its temporary nature, meaning it transitions to closure upon achieving its objectives. Closure is an essential phase in the lifecycle of a project. It involves completing all project activities, evaluating performance, and reallocating resources. This phase ensures that the project team assesses the project's outcomes against the original objectives and documents any lessons learned for future reference. After completing a research initiative, the project team would compile a final report, hold a debrief meeting, and then release team members to other tasks.

Closure also involves handling any remaining administrative tasks, such as releasing financial resources, closing contracts, and delivering the final product or service to the customer. The project team should establish clear criteria for project completion early in the planning phase to avoid ambiguity during closure. By doing so, the team can make sure a smooth transition without lingering issues. With our new office building project, the team needs to fulfill contractual obligations, hand over the finished building, and archive project documents for closure.

The Role of a Project Manager

A project manager plays a crucial role in ensuring the success of projects by aligning goals with organizational strategy and stakeholder expectations. This involves meticulous planning, efficient execution, and effective closure of projects. The responsibilities of a project manager begin from the project's start and extend to its completion, encompassing several key tasks.

First, project managers need to develop a comprehensive project plan that outlines the scope, timeline, resources required, and potential risks. The plan is a roadmap that guides the team through the project phases. The plan ensures all activities align with the project's objectives and organizational goals, facilitating smooth progress towards the desired outcomes. Managing these aspects requires strong leadership skills.

Leadership is paramount for project managers, as they often serve as the cornerstone of the project team. Effective leaders inspire and motivate their teams, fostering a collaborative environment where everyone works towards common goals. By setting clear expectations and providing regular feedback, project managers make sure team members stay focused and engaged. Leadership also involves making critical decisions and resolving conflicts, which can arise from competing priorities or different perspectives within the team.

Communication is another vital skill for project managers. Clear and consistent communication helps in disseminating important information, setting expectations, and addressing concerns. Effective communication not only keeps team members informed, but also fosters transparency and trust among stakeholders. Regular meetings, updates, and reports are essential tools that project managers used to keep open lines of communication.

Negotiation is also an integral part of a project manager's toolkit. Whether it's negotiating deadlines, budgets, or resource allocation, project managers must find a balance between the needs of the project and the constraints imposed by stakeholders. Successful negotiation requires the ability to understand different viewpoints, find common ground, and propose solutions that satisfy all parties involved. This skill is important when dealing with suppliers, clients, and other external entities whose cooperation is crucial for project success.

Risk management is another critical area where project managers play a pivotal role. Every project faces uncertainties that might derail its progress. Identifying risks early and developing mitigation strategies can prevent minor issues from escalating into major problems. Project managers must assess and reassess risks, adapting their plans as necessary to discuss new challenges. Being proactive helps to maintain the project's timeline, even when unforeseen events happen.

Understanding and managing stakeholder expectations is critical. Stakeholders, including clients, sponsors, and team members, have varying needs and priorities that can sometimes conflict. Effective engagement strategies involve listening to stakeholders, understanding their concerns, and addressing them in a manner that aligns with the project's objectives. By keeping stakeholders engaged and informed, project managers can mitigate risks associated with conflicting demands and foster support for the project.

Project managers also act as problem-solvers, navigating through unexpected challenges and uncertainties. This requires being flexible and taking initiative. When faced with obstacles, project managers must quickly analyze the situation, find workable solutions, and carry out the most effective course of action. Their ability to guide teams through turbulent times without losing sight of the project's goals is a testament to their problem-solving skills.

For instance, consider a scenario where a project encounters a significant delay because of unforeseen technical issues. A proficient project manager would first assess the impact of the delay on the project's overall timeline and objectives. They would then explore various options to mitigate the delay, such as reallocating resources, adjusting deadlines, or finding alternative solutions to the technical problem. Throughout this process, the project manager would communicate with stakeholders, keeping them informed about the steps being taken to resolve the issue and any potential adjustments to the project plan.

Besides these skills, project managers need a deep understanding of the industry they are working in. Different industries have unique challenges and requirements, and familiarity with these nuances enables project managers to tailor their approaches. Project management in the construction industry involves stricter safety regulations and coordination with multiple contractors, while project management in IT emphasizes software development methodologies and rapid technological changes.

To illustrate prizing industry-specific knowledge, imagine a project manager overseeing a large-scale software implementation. The project manager should stay updated on the latest software technologies, know how to integrate new systems with existing ones, and be aware of potential cybersecurity risks. This knowledge allows the project manager to make informed decisions that enhance the project's chances of success.

Successful project managers seek to improve their skills and knowledge. This commitment to professional development ensures that they stay effective in their roles despite the developing nature of the project management landscape. Staying updated with the latest project management methodologies, tools, and certifications, such as the PMP (Project Management Professional), equips project managers with the ability needed to handle complex projects.

For instance, taking part in workshops, attending conferences, or pursuing advanced certifications can give project managers with new insights and techniques that they can apply to their projects. Connecting with other professionals in the same field provides chances to learn from their experiences and exchange helpful strategies.

Project Management Lifecycle

Understanding the stages of the project management lifecycle is critical for ensuring the success of any project, from initiation to closure. These stages give a structured approach that helps project managers and teams navigate through complex tasks. There are five essential phases in this lifecycle: initiation, planning, execution, monitoring, and closure. Each phase plays a pivotal role in guiding a project to its successful completion.

The first phase, initiation, sets the foundation for a project. This stage involves identifying and selecting projects that align with strategic organizational objectives. In this stage, it is important to outline clearly the objectives, goals, and expected outcomes of the project. The project manager conducts a feasibility assessment to decide if the project is practical and worthwhile. By aligning all stakeholders on common goals and expectations, the initiation phase establishes a clear direction and ensures everyone agrees. Tools, such as the project charter, which outlines key objectives, stakeholders, and first estimates of time and budget, are essential here. (Coursera, 2022)

Once the team starts a project and deems it workable, it moves into the planning phase. During this phase, the team develops a comprehensive project plan that details how they will achieve the project's goals. It encompasses scheduling, resource allocation, budgeting, and risk management. A well-crafted plan expects potential risks and establishes mitigation strategies to discuss them. Tools like Gantt charts are used to map out the timeline of tasks and milestones, providing a visual representation of the project's schedule. Effective planning also involves setting up communication protocols to make sure consistent and clear updates among team members and stakeholders. Holding a kick-off meeting at the start of this phase can help solidify understanding and commitment from all involved parties. (Coursera, 2022)

With a thorough plan in place, the project enters the execution phase. This is where the actual work creates the project's final products. The team carries out the tasks outlined in the project plan, which require strong team management and coordination. It's essential to keep focus, manage quality, and stick to the predetermined schedule as closely as possible. Regular status meetings and progress reports keep everyone informed and engaged. Tools such as burndown charts and change requests help track progress and manage any alterations needed to stay on course. Monitoring and controlling processes run with execution, ensuring that the project remains aligned with its objectives. This includes tracking key performance indicators, managing risks as they arise, and making necessary adjustments to keep the project on track. (Atlassian, 2024)

The monitoring and controlling phase overlaps with the execution phase, but its primary focus is on measuring the project's performance against the plan. During this phase, the project manager tracks completing tasks, monitors costs, and ensures that the project stays within scope. Effective monitoring provides insights into whether the project is progressing as expected or if corrective actions are required. Regular check-ins and performance reviews help preempt potential issues before they escalate. By comparing actual progress with planned progress, the project manager can discuss deviations and. Tools like dashboards and performance reports play a crucial role in this phase by offering real-time data and insights. (Coursera, 2022)

The closure phase marks the end of the project lifecycle. This stage involves wrapping up all project activities, delivering the final product or service, and evaluating the project outcomes. It's important to conduct a retrospective review to document lessons learned and gather feedback from all stakeholders. This information is invaluable for improving future projects. Closure also involves completing any outstanding tasks, releasing project resources, and getting formal acceptance from the client or project sponsor. Proper documentation of the project's successes and challenges ensures better planning and execution in later projects. Celebrating completing the project and acknowledging the efforts of the team can enhance morale and foster a positive working environment for future collaborations. (Coursera, 2022)

Final Thoughts

In this chapter, we've laid the groundwork for understanding project management by exploring its definition and essential characteristics. We've distinguished projects from ongoing operations, emphasizing their temporary nature, clear objectives, and specific constraints. We discussed the crucial role of stakeholders and the variability in project size, scope, and complexity. By understanding these fundamental aspects, you are better equipped to grasp the broader concepts of project management, which is vital for anyone preparing for the PMP exam.

As we move forward, keep these core principles in mind. Whether you're managing a minor task or leading a large-scale initiative, these foundational elements will guide your planning and execution processes. Remember, the key to successful project management lies in balancing time, cost, and scope while engaging stakeholders and adapting to challenges. With this foundational knowledge, you're well on your way to mastering the art of project management and advancing in your career.

Reference List

Alexander, M. (2023, June 26). *What is a project manager? The lead role for project success* . CIO. https://

www.cio.com/article/230682/what-is-a-project-manager-the-lead-role-for-project-success.html

Atlassian. (2024). *A Guide to the Project Life Cycle: Exploring the 5 Phases* . Atlassian. https://www.atlassian.com/work-management/project-management/project-life-cycle

Coursera. (2022). *4 Phases of the Project Management Lifecycle Explained* . Coursera. https://www.coursera.org/articles/project-management-lifecycle

Eamonn McGuinness. (2023, March 21). *What Are the Characteristics of a Project?* BrightWork.com. https://www.brightwork.com/blog/what-are-the-characteristics-of-a-project

What is the difference between projects and operations | Project Management Basics . (n.d.). Projectinsight.com. https://projectinsight.com/project-management-basics/projects-and-operations

wrike. (2024). *What Are the Roles and Responsibilities of a Project Manager?* Wrike. https://www.wrike.com/project-management-guide/faq/what-are-the-roles-and-responsibilities-of-a-project-manager/

Chapter 2 - Project Integration Management

Project Integration Management facilitates seamless coordination among project elements. When managing a project, it's easy to focus on individual tasks and lose sight of how they fit into the bigger picture. Effective integration management prevents this by ensuring all aspects are in harmony. Avoid conflicts and issues by synchronizing different project parts.

This chapter will cover the essential elements of Project Integration Management that are crucial for project success. Start with the fundamentals of a project charter, the building block of your project. The training will cover understanding how to find and engage stakeholders early on, emphasizing communication strategies tailored to diverse needs. The next chapter will cover carrying out the project plan, overseeing team performance, and making sure the work meets high standards. You'll learn about monitoring project progress and managing changes. You'll have a complete grasp on coordinating project aspects efficiently by the end of the chapter, guaranteeing successful delivery.

Developing Project Charter

Developing a thorough project charter is essential for establishing a strong project foundation. The project charter is an important document that formally allows a project. It outlines the project's objectives and identifies key stakeholders, ensuring that everyone involved understands the project's purpose and goals from the outset. This foundational document functions as a road map, guiding the project team and stakeholders through the project's lifecycle.

To create a strong project charter, start by identifying all relevant stakeholders. Stakeholders include anyone who has an interest or influence on the project, such as sponsors, clients, team members, and regulatory bodies. It is important to identify and document stakeholders early in order to communicate and involve them in the project. By understanding who the stakeholders are and what their interests and expectations might be, the project manager can tailor communication strategies to meet diverse needs and keep everyone aligned.

Once stakeholders are identified, establishing project requirements and resource estimates at a high level becomes crucial. The elements give a concise project summary with necessary resources. Having this clarity in the project's initiation phase streamlines planning efforts, making it easier to allocate resources appropriately and set realistic timelines.

SMART criteria should outline high-level project requirements—specific, measurable, achievable, realistic, and time bound. This method ensures that the requirements are clear and attainable, providing a strong framework for project success. Rather than making a broad statement like "enhance customer service," a SMART aim would be to "decrease customer response time by 20% in six months."

It is important to be proactive in communication once you have identified the people involved and the things they need. Effective methods to find and engage stakeholders early can involve stakeholder analysis tools and techniques, such as RACI matrices (Responsible, Accountable, Consulted, and Informed) or stakeholder mapping. Using these tools allows the project manager to categorize stakeholders based on their level of influence and interest in the project. By doing so, the project team can rank communication efforts and ensure that they keep critical stakeholders informed and engaged throughout the project.

When documenting stakeholder information, important to include contact details, roles and responsibilities, and preferred communication methods. Regular updates and transparent communication are key to maintaining stakeholder support and mitigating potential conflicts or misunderstandings. Setting up dedicated communication channels, like regular status meetings or project management software, assists ongoing dialogue and collaboration.

The project charter requires a critical approval process to establish a solid project foundation. This process involves getting formal sign-off from key stakeholders and governance bodies, which signifies their commitment and support for the project. Understanding the steps needed for obtaining approval can vary depending on the organization's governance structures. Some organizations require approval from a steering committee, while others might involve executive leadership or external regulators.

Governance structures have a significant impact on the speed and efficiency of the project initiation process. Understanding these structures helps the project manager navigate any bureaucratic hurdles and expedites the approval process. Standardized procedures, such as "Project in a Box" toolkits, can assist busy project managers in tailoring governance frameworks to fit their specific needs. These toolkits give guidelines on how much governance is required, find mandatory decision gates, and offer templates for essential documents (Alie, 2015).

An effective governance model should balance strictness and adaptability. Overzealous governance can alienate stakeholders and slow down progress, while insufficient governance may lead to a lack of accountability and nuclear decision-making paths. By establishing a baseline of key governance elements based on project scope, complexity, risk, and importance to the organization, project managers can develop a governance framework that supports project success without unnecessary complications.

Once approved, stakeholders can share the project charter to ensure transparency and alignment with project expectations and commitments. The charter also serves as a persuasive tool to show the project's value proposition, helping to secure stakeholder agreement and excitement. Detailed in the charter might include project objectives and constraints, key stakeholders, risks identified, benefits of the project, and a general overview of the budget and timeline (Wrike, 2019).

Directing and Managing Project Work

Effective leadership and management of the project during execution are crucial for smooth progress and attainment. This involves transforming the project plan into actionable tasks, managing deliverables with a focus on quality, leading project teams through effective communication, and maintaining proper documentation.

Breaking down the project plan into smaller parts makes it more actionable. The project plan should break down each task into smaller, manageable parts and clearly define specific goals, timelines, and responsibilities assigned to team members. As a project manager, it's essential to oversee this process, ensuring everyone understands their roles and how their work contributes to the project's success. Creating detailed schedules, using tools like Gantt charts or Kanban boards, can help visualize tasks and track progress. Regular check-ins and updates ensure tasks are being completed on time and promptly address any issues.

Enhancing team performance is an important duty of the project manager. An effective project manager recognizes that the success of the project largely depends on the team's performance. Creating a motivating and valued environment for team members is crucial. Managers can achieve this by setting clear expectations, providing the resources, and offering regular feedback. Celebrating small wins along the way can also boost morale and keep the team motivated.

Quality management is key in overseeing project outcomes from creation to delivery. To complete tasks alone is not sufficient. Implementing quality assurance processes ensures that each deliverable meets the required standards before completing. This might involve regular testing, reviews, and inspections at various stages of the project. By prioritizing quality, you minimize the risk of rework, save time and resources, and enhance stakeholder satisfaction with the final product.

Inclusive communication and collaboration are key methods for effective project team leadership. Open and transparent communication facilitates the building of trust and alignment among team members. It's important to establish regular communication channels, such as weekly meetings, update emails, and collaborative online platforms, where team members can share updates, ask questions, and give feedback. Encouraging an open-door policy where team members feel comfortable raising concerns or suggesting improvements can lead to better project outcomes.

Inclusive communication involves recognizing and valuing diverse perspectives in your team. Different team members bring unique skills and viewpoints to the table, which can enhance problem-solving and innovation. As a project manager, actively promote a culture of inclusivity by encouraging everyone to contribute ideas and take part in discussions. This not only improves decision making but also fosters a sense of belonging and commitment among team members.

Proper documentation ensures transparency and accountability in project execution. Proper documentation records what was done, who did it, and when it was completed. This is important in complex projects where multiple stakeholders are involved. Well-maintained records help track progress, find bottlenecks, and ensure smooth handovers if team members change. It also serves as a reference for future projects, providing valuable lessons learned and best practices.

Establish a structured method from the start for efficient documentation. This includes using standardized templates for reports, meeting minutes, and other documents. It is also essential to update these documents regularly and store them in a centralized location accessible to all stakeholders. Tools like project management software can help automate and streamline this process, making it easier to maintain accurate and up-to-date records.

Monitoring and Controlling Project Work

It is essential to track and measure project performance to make sure it aligns with the project management plan. It entails a thorough strategy that employs diverse techniques to evaluate performance, analyze discrepancies, communicate results to stakeholders, and manage conflicting constraints.

Regular status reports are highly effective for assessing project performance. They provide a snapshot of the project's current state by comparing actual progress with planned milestones. Common tools include Gantt charts and dashboards that offer visual representations of the project's trajectory. Project managers rely on these tools to spot discrepancies early and make informed decisions to keep the project on track.

Earned Value Management (EVM) is vital for performance measurement to status reports. EVM combines scope, schedule, and cost data to generate metrics that reflect project health. Key indicators such as Planned Value (PV), Earned Value (EV), and Actual Cost (AC) give project managers insights into schedule and budget performance. For instance, if EV is less than PV, the project is behind schedule. Conversely, if AC exceeds EV, the project is over budget. By continuously monitoring this metric, managers can promptly find issues and implement corrective actions.

Another crucial aspect of performance measurement is variance analysis. This process involves comparing the baseline plan with the actual performance to find deviations. Variances can occur in multiple dimensions, including scope, time, and cost. By examining these variances, project managers can determine the root causes and assess their impact on the project's overall objectives. For example, a time variance might be because of unforeseen delays or resource shortages. Once project managers identify the root causes, they can make timely interventions, such as reallocating resources or adjusting timelines to mitigate the impact.

It is crucial to communicate project performance and transparently to stakeholders. Regular communication ensures that all parties stay informed about the project's status and any potential risks or changes. Effective communication strategies include holding stakeholder meetings, distributing detailed performance reports, and using collaboration tools to foster ongoing dialogue. Clarity and transparency in communications build trust and makes sure that stakeholders agree, reducing the risk of misunderstandings and misaligned expectations.

It is essential to take project constraints such as time, cost, and quality into consideration. These constraints, often referred to as the triple constraint, require careful management to achieve project success. Time refers to how long the project will take, cost refers to the amount of money needed, and quality refers to the standards that the deliverables must meet. Managing these constraints involves making trade-offs, as changes in one constraint can affect the others.

For example, when a project experiences a delay, project managers may have to either allocate more resources, resulting in higher costs, or reduce the scope to adhere to the original timeline. Conversely, enhancing quality must require more time and money, affecting the overall budget and schedule. The key is to find a balance that satisfies project objectives while keeping stakeholders' needs in mind.

To handle these conflicting demands, use a project management dashboard. Dashboards offer real-time visibility into key metrics, such as schedule, cost, and scope. With this information, project managers can quickly find emerging issues and adjust the triple constraint accordingly to prevent minor problems from becoming major obstacles. For example, managers can easily see who is overloaded with tasks and reallocate work to ensure balanced resource distribution by utilizing a workload page with color-coded charts.

Performing Integrated Change Control

Effectively managing changes throughout the project lifecycle is crucial for smooth project delivery and minimizing disruptions. Employing a systematic approach to change management can mitigate the risk of project delays, budget overruns, and scope creep, which could all pose a threat to project success.

First, it is crucial to have a clearly defined change control process. The process begins with identifying the need for change. This identification can come from anyone involved in the project, including team members, stakeholders, or even external partners. Once identified, the next step is to document the change and ask formally. This documentation includes a change ask form that outlines the proposed change, its rationale, and the expected benefits. Keeping a comprehensive record of these requests is vital, as it aids in conflict resolution and ensures transparency (Westland, 2022).

In the second step, we evaluate how the proposed change will affect the project's scope, timeline, and budget. It's essential to conduct a rigorous analysis to understand how the change will affect the overall project. Project managers need to ask how changes will affect our work. What additional resources will be required? Will the schedule need to change? Evaluating these factors helps in making informed decisions about whether to proceed with the change (Lawler, 2023).

Once complete, we should present the findings from the impact assessment to a Change Control Board (CCB). The CCB comprises key stakeholders and subject experts who review the change ask. They consider the change's alignment with project goals and its potential risks and benefits. The CCB then approves, rejects, or defers the change. This formal approval process helps maintain the integrity of the project by ensuring that matter experts thoroughly scrutinize all changes before implementation (Lawler, 2023).

Once we approve the changes, the next step involves planning the implementation. This phase includes updating project documents, reallocating resources, and changing timelines. It is essential to communicate these updates clearly and promptly to all relevant stakeholders and team members. Effective communication ensures everyone agrees and reduces the chances of misunderstandings or confusion. Regular update meetings and detailed status reports track this process, promoting a culture of transparency and inclusiveness.

It is essential to manage and prevent scope creep, which refers to the uncontrolled growth of the project scope beyond its initial boundaries. Scope creep can lead to significant delays, budget overruns, and compromised project quality. A vigilant approach to handling change requests, coupled with robust project scope control mechanisms, helps maintain focus and alignment with the project's original objectives. By systematically evaluating, approving, and implementing changes, project managers can navigate the challenges while keeping the project on track (Lawler, 2023).

Extensively documenting the entire change management process is important. It is important to maintain detailed records of each change request, including reasons for the change, impact assessments, approval status, and implementation steps, meticulously. This documentation serves multiple purposes: it provides a historical record for future reference, aids in conflict resolution, and supports continuous improvement in managing changes.

Equally important are successful tactics for conveying allowed modifications. Once a change is approved, efficient communication of the modification to all stakeholders and the project team is a must. Clear communication aids in setting the right expectations and ensures everyone understands their roles and responsibilities concerning the change. Using various communication channels, such as emails, meetings, and project management software, can help disseminate information effectively. Addressing questions promptly helps to build trust and foster collaboration among team members and stakeholders.

By using proven methods to improve the process, we can successfully implement change. One such practice is adopting an agile mindset, which involves breaking down changes into smaller, manageable tasks and implementing them incrementally. This approach allows for faster adaptations and minimizes the risk of overwhelming the project team. Testing and validating substantial changes within a controlled environment before full-scale implementation can also find potential issues early and make sure smoother transitions.

Setting priorities is another crucial approach to follow. Prioritizing changes based on their potential impact on project goals and success is essential because not all changes are equally important. By focusing on high-priority changes first, we ensure that we promptly address the most significant improvements, contributing to the overall success of the project.

During the change management process, involving stakeholders is essential. Stakeholders' input and feedback are invaluable in understanding the broader implications of changes and ensuring that the adjustments meet their expectations. Involving them in decision-making fosters a sense of ownership and accountability, which can positively influence the project's outcome.

Final Insights

In this chapter, we explored the vital role of coordinating all project elements for successful completion. We began with the creation of a project charter, which acts as the project's foundation by outlining objectives and identifying key stakeholders. Emphasizing stakeholder engagement and clear communication, we discussed how these elements help align everyone involved and set realistic expectations. We highlighted the importance of clarifying project requirements and securing necessary approvals to establish a strong governance framework.

While progressing, we analyzed methods for guiding and overseeing project tasks, emphasizing task breakdown and team performance through leadership and quality management. We stress the significance of consistently documenting every aspect of the project to promote transparency and accountability. By monitoring and controlling project progress and employing integrated change control processes, we can manage changes smoothly and prevent scope creep. Together, these practices make sure that projects remain on track, stay within budget, and meet their intended goals, ultimately leading to successful project outcomes.

Reference List

Alie, S. S. (2015). *Project Governance* . Project Management Institute. https://www.pmi.org/learning/library/project-governance-critical-success-9945

BLINK. (2023, September 6). *10 tips for effective & successful project management | Blink* . Www.joinblink.com. https://www.joinblink.com/intelligence/successful-project-management

Increase Project Team Effectiveness - Step-by-Step . (n.d.). Www.pmi.org. https://www.pmi.org/learning/library/increase-project-team-effectiveness-steps-6070

Lawler, B. (2023, October 16). *Managing Project Changes: Implementing Scope Change Requests* . DSM | Digital School of Marketing; DSM | Digital School of Marketing. https://digitalschoolofmarketing.co.za/project-management/managing-project-changes-implementing-scope-change-requests/

Oguz, A. (2022, October 10). *1.3 Project Constraints* . Pressbooks.ulib.csuohio.edu. https://pressbooks.ulib.csuohio.edu/project-management-navigating-the-complexity/chapter/1-3-project-constraints/

Westland, J. (2022, January 17). *The Triple Constraint in Project Management: Time, Scope & Cost* . ProjectManager.com. https://www.projectmanager.com/blog/triple-constraint-project-management-time-scope-cost

Westland, J. (2022, February 14). *What is change control in project management?* ProjectManager.com. https://www.projectmanager.com/blog/what-is-change-control-in-project-management

wrike. (2019). *What is a Project Charter in Project Management?* Wrike.com. https://www.wrike.com/project-management-guide/faq/what-is-a-project-charter-in-project-management/

Chapter 3 - Scope Management

Managing the scope of a project is key to ensuring its success. To ensure the success of a project, it is key to manage its scope actively. This chapter explores how effective scope management can prevent scope creep, which can lead to project delays and increased costs. It emphasizes the importance of clear communication with stakeholders and maintaining a focus on the project's objectives.

Throughout this chapter, you will learn various techniques, and strategies for managing project scope. This chapter discusses the importance of gathering and documenting stakeholder requirements. It also explores methods for breaking down the scope into manageable components using tools like the Work Breakdown Structure (WBS). The course also teaches practical methods to validate and control the project's scope, which helps ensure that the project's outcomes meet the expectations of those involved. By the end of this chapter, you should have a solid understanding of how to keep your project on track and within its defined boundaries.

Collecting Requirements

Understanding stakeholder needs and expectations is crucial for defining project scope effectively. When we hear and value stakeholders' input, they are more likely to support and engage with the project's objectives. This section focuses on how to identify stakeholders, gather their insights, and document this information to lay a strong foundation for your project's scope.

First, stakeholder analysis involves identifying all relevant stakeholders and understanding their needs and influence on the project. Stakeholders can include anyone from clients and users to team members and investors—anyone who has an interest or investment in the project's outcome. Begin by brainstorming with key team members to list potential stakeholders. Always consider both internal stakeholders, like project team members, and external stakeholders, such as customers and suppliers, to ensure no critical voices are missing from the analysis.

Engaging stakeholders early in the project lifecycle can significantly mitigate risks and align expectations. Early engagement provides clarity about the project's goals from different perspectives, helping to avoid conflicts later. Techniques such as interviews and surveys are invaluable tools for gathering deep insights into what stakeholders expect from the project. Interviewing allows for real-time interaction and follow-up questions, which can reveal nuanced needs and concerns that might not come up with written surveys. Surveys can reach a wider audience and provide quantitative data that is easier to analyze systematically.

Different techniques serve various stakeholder preferences, maximizing engagement and ensuring comprehensive feedback. Some stakeholders may prefer face-to-face meetings or phone calls for a personal touch, while others might opt for online surveys because of time constraints. Offering multiple ways for stakeholders to provide input increases the likelihood of full participation. For example, providing both digital surveys and scheduled interview slots ensures flexibility and accommodates diverse schedules and comfort levels.

Clear documentation of stakeholder needs and expectations prevents miscommunication later in the project lifecycle. The project team should accurately record and share every piece of feedback. This transparency ensures everyone agrees and reduces the risk of misinterpretations as the project progresses. Documentation can take many forms, such as detailed meeting notes, survey result summaries, and stakeholder requirement matrices. These documents should be readily accessible to the project team for ongoing reference.

Stakeholder analysis also requires political astuteness and strategic thinking. Understanding the attributes and interrelationships among stakeholders helps in planning how to manage their expectations and gain their support. For instance, knowing which stakeholders have significant influence over project decisions can guide prioritization efforts and communication strategies. Strategic planning includes not just understanding individual needs but also identifying potential coalitions of support or sources of opposition within the stakeholder group.

We should not see collecting and analyzing stakeholder feedback as a onetime effort, but as an ongoing activity throughout the project. Stakeholder expectations can develop, especially in long-term projects. Regular check-ins and updates ensure we capture and address any shifts in expectations promptly. For example, quarterly reviews of stakeholder feedback can help identify trends and adjust project plans proactively, reducing the chance of unexpected issues down the line.

Prioritizing stakeholder needs helps focus efforts on where they matter most. Since not all stakeholders' requirements can be met equally, it's essential to distinguish between critical needs and nice-to-haves. Using tools like a priority matrix can aid in this assessment, helping the project team allocate resources efficiently. The project team should address critical needs first to maintain stakeholder satisfaction and project viability.

Last, documenting the processes and decisions made based on stakeholder feedback creates a valuable repository of knowledge for current and future projects. People involved can use this repository to observe successful strategies and encountered challenges, thus promoting ongoing improvement in managing stakeholders. Properly documented decisions also provide accountability and a clear trail of thought processes for project decisions, which can be crucial during audits or reviews.

Defining Scope

To accomplish a project, one needs to have a clear definition of what they need to do and what they will deliver.

This begins with a well-defined scope statement, which sets the stage for guiding project execution and managing stakeholder expectations. A comprehensive scope statement both includes a list of what will be part of the project and clearly defines what will not be included. This clarity helps all parties involved understand the project's limitations and focus on the expected outcomes.

A well-defined scope statement sets clear boundaries that guide project execution. It includes detailed descriptions of the project's deliverables, tasks, and milestones. By outlining every component, team members gain a thorough understanding of their responsibilities, contributing to smoother project execution. Defining the scope gives project managers a framework to track progress and ensure that all activities align with the initial plan. For example, in a construction project, the scope statement might detail the number of floors in a building, the materials to be used, and specific safety standards to follow. Such specificity keeps the project on track and within budget.

Clearly stating exclusions helps manage stakeholder expectations and prevents scope creep. When extra features or tasks are added to a project without proper authorization, it can become challenging to manage stakeholders' expectations. This can lead to scope creep, causing delays and increased costs. Specifying what is not included allows project managers to better control stakeholder demands and maintain a focus on the agreed-upon objectives. For instance, if a software development project does not include certain functionalities like real-time data analytics, project managers should communicate this exclusion at the outset. Doing so ensures stakeholders know these features will not be part of the current project phase, reducing the risk of unexpected demands later.

Defined acceptance criteria provide measurable benchmarks against project outcomes. Acceptance criteria define the conditions that deliverables must meet to be complete and satisfactory. These criteria serve as the project's quality standards, ensuring that the final product meets the stakeholders' requirements. For example, in a marketing campaign project, acceptance criteria might include achieving a specific number of social media engagements or reaching a defined target audience. These measurable benchmarks help us objectively assess whether the project goals have been fulfilled, leading to smoother sign-offs and fewer disputes regarding the quality of the deliverables.

Regularly reviewing scope against progress can highlight potential misalignments. Consistent monitoring and assessment of the project scope relative to actual progress helps identify discrepancies early on. This proactive approach enables project managers to address issues before they escalate, ensuring the project stays on track. For instance, in an event planning project, regular reviews might reveal that vendor contracts do not align with the initially defined scope, prompting timely renegotiations to avoid last-minute surprises. Such vigilance minimizes risks and supports the overall success of the project.

Creating Work Breakdown Structure (WBS)

In project management, breaking down deliverables into manageable components is vital for successful execution. This technique, known as the Work Breakdown Structure (WBS), enhances the team's understanding of tasks and responsibilities. By decomposing the overall project scope into smaller, more digestible parts, you make it easier for team members to grasp their specific roles and contributions.

A well-structured WBS brings organization and clarity, which directly affects resource management and tracking. When we clearly outline each component of the project, assigning tasks becomes more straightforward, and we simplify monitoring progress. By seeing how individual tasks interconnect and contribute to the overall aim, teams can work more cohesively and efficiently.

Determining the right level of detail or granularity within a WBS is crucial. If the breakdown is too broad, the team might overlook critical details, which can lead to confusion and potential project delays. If you break down the tasks too finely, the WBS could become unwieldy and overly complex. The goal is to find a balance where tasks are comprehensive enough to cover all necessary work but still manageable for the team members responsible for them.

Documentation within a WBS serves a critical role in clarifying deliverables and requirements for each task. Detailed documentation provides a road map that guides team members through what needs to be done, by whom, and by when. It helps prevent miscommunication and ensures everyone agrees. Clear documentation allows for better planning, scheduling, and resource allocation, reducing misunderstandings and errors throughout the project lifecycle.

Leveraging technology can significantly streamline the development and updates of a WBS. Various software tools help create and maintaining a WBS, making the process more efficient and accurate. Gantt charts, Kanban boards, and specialized project management software can automate many aspects of WBS creation and maintenance, ensuring that they capture and communicate every change effectively. These technologies offer visual representations that can enhance comprehension and provide real-time updates on task progress and project status.

Using these tools not only makes the WBS more dynamic but also allows for better tracking of progress and quicker adaptation to changes. For example, Gantt charts offer a timeline view of tasks and their dependencies, making it easier to see the sequence of activities and identify any potential bottlenecks. Kanban boards provide a flexible way to visualize work items and track their status through different stages of completion. Such tools facilitate communication among team members and stakeholders, ensuring everyone is aware of the project's current state and what needs to be prioritized next.

Creating a WBS involves several steps, starting with identifying the main deliverables of the project. Once the overarching goals are clear, these deliverables must be broken down into smaller components, tasks, and subtasks. Each level of decomposition adds more detail, helping to paint a clearer picture of what is required to complete the project successfully.

For instance, if the project is to develop a mobile application, the main deliverable would be the fully functional app. We can break this down into modules such as user interface design, backend development, testing, and deployment. We can further break down each module into specific tasks. User interface design could involve tasks, such as designing basic layouts, improving the overall user experience, and programming the interface. Backend development could include setting up the server, creating databases, and integrating APIs. By continuing to break down each area into smaller tasks, the entire scope of work becomes much more understandable and manageable.

The key components of a WBS include primary deliverables, work packages, and tasks. Primary deliverables represent the major outcomes or objectives of the project. Work packages are the building blocks within the WBS, each containing a collection of tasks that need to be completed to achieve a specific deliverable. Tasks are individual units of work that form part of a work package, providing detailed steps required for completion.

Using a WBS helps in cost estimation, task scheduling, and resource allocation. By having a clear outline of what needs to be done, project managers can estimate the time and resources required for each task more accurately. Project managers can use this help to budget and ensure that they allocate resources to where they are needed most. Project managers can estimate the time and resources required for each task more accurately, which aids in budgeting and ensures that resources are allocated where they are needed most. This makes scheduling easier because it clearly outlines dependencies between tasks, allowing for better planning of timelines and deadlines.

Besides aiding in project execution, a WBS is essential for project control. It establishes benchmarks against which progress can be measured. Regularly comparing actual performance against the WBS allows for early detection of deviations from the plan, enabling corrective actions to be taken before small issues become major problems. This proactive approach can help keep the project on track and within its defined scope, ultimately leading to a successful outcome.

Validating and Controlling Scope

Ensuring that a project's scope remains aligned with stakeholder expectations and project objectives throughout its lifecycle is crucial for successful project management. A well-aligned scope ensures that the project stays on track, within budget, and meets the intended outcomes. Here, we delve into strategies to maintain this alignment effectively.

Consistent validation with stakeholders is fundamental to ensuring that project outputs meet requirements. This involves ongoing communication and engagement with stakeholders at every stage of the project. During initial planning, it's important to gather comprehensive requirements through methods such as interviews, workshops, and surveys. These interactions should continue throughout the project to confirm that the work being done aligns with stakeholders' needs and expectations. Regular meetings, status updates, and reviews serve as checkpoints to validate that the project remains on course. By involving stakeholders in these reviews, we can identify and address any discrepancies or changes in requirements promptly, preventing misalignment and rework.

Proactively tracking additional requests is another critical aspect of scope management. In many projects, new ideas and additional requirements emerge as the work progresses. While some of these requests may add value, others can lead to scope creep—a major risk factor for project delays and cost overruns. Scope creep occurs when the project scope expands beyond its original boundaries without corresponding adjustments in time, cost, and resources. To handle this, establish a formal change control process. This process should involve documenting, evaluating, and either approving or rejecting all additional requests, taking into consideration their impact on the project's timeline, budget, and objectives. Implementing a formal change control process helps maintain control over the project scope by ensuring that only necessary and beneficial changes are incorporated.

Regular scope audits play a pivotal role in ensuring alignment with initial objectives. These audits involve a thorough review of the project deliverables against the defined scope statement and work breakdown structure (WBS). By conducting these audits periodically, project managers can verify that the work completed corresponds to what they originally planned and agreed upon. If project managers find any deviations, they can promptly take corrective actions. Audits also provide an opportunity to reassess the scope by considering any changes in project direction or external factors, ensuring continued relevance and alignment with stakeholder expectations. These assessments help to identify potential issues early and provide a structured way to address them.

Capturing insights into scope-related challenges is essential for improving future scope planning efforts. Every project presents unique challenges and learning opportunities. Documenting these experiences provides valuable feedback for refining scope management practices. For instance, if a particular type of scope change frequently causes issues, this insight can inform more robust planning and control in future projects. Similarly, understanding which stakeholder engagement strategies were most effective can enhance future communication plans. Encourage the project team to contribute to these lessons learned sessions, creating a comprehensive repository of knowledge that benefits the organization beyond the current project.

Besides these specific strategies, it is helpful to establish clear guidelines for scope management. Setting expectations early about what makes up the project scope can mitigate future conflicts. Both the project team and stakeholders need to understand the boundaries of the project and what will not be included. This clarity helps prevent misunderstandings and disagreements later in the project lifecycle. Gaining formal approval of the scope from key stakeholders before the project begins is vital to securing support and commitment.

Reviewing requirements with stakeholders confirms alignment with their needs. When gathering requirements initially, involving the relevant stakeholders in reviewing and validating these requirements is crucial. This step ensures that the captured requirements accurately reflect what the stakeholders expect from the project. Gaining stakeholder approval at this stage prevents potential project delays caused by misunderstandings or incomplete requirements. It also builds a sense of ownership and accountability among stakeholders, enhancing their support throughout the project.

Communicate effectively with the project team and stakeholders to maintain alignment. Clear and open communication channels are essential for managing expectations, resolving conflicts, and addressing scope-related issues proactively. Regular updates, progress reports, and stakeholder meetings keep everyone informed and engaged. Maintaining transparency in communication helps build trust and ensures prompt addressing of any concerns or changes, thus preserving the integrity of the project's scope.

Empower the project team with the authority and resources necessary to decide within their scope of work. Encouraging collaboration and providing adequate support ensures that team members understand and adhere to the project scope. Empowered teams can respond quickly to challenges and make informed decisions that align with the project's objectives. Providing training and resources to enhance their understanding of scope management practices further strengthens their ability to maintain scope alignment.

Conduct scope verification to ensure project deliverables meet predefined acceptance criteria. This process involves comparing the completed work against the agreed-upon criteria to confirm that it fulfills stakeholder expectations. Scope verification serves as a quality check, ensuring that the project is on track to deliver the intended outcomes. The project team can rectify any discrepancies identified during this process before the final delivery, ensuring stakeholder satisfaction.

Learning from lessons learned throughout the project lifecycle is continuous and integral to improving scope management practices. Document feedback and incorporate it into future projects to enhance outcomes. Continuous learning and adaptation are essential for staying ahead of potential challenges and optimizing project performance.

Summary and Reflections

In this chapter, we delved into the importance of defining and managing project scope. By thoroughly understanding stakeholder needs and expectations, you can lay a solid foundation for your project's success. Through techniques like stakeholder analysis, interviews, and surveys, it's possible to gather comprehensive insights that guide your project's direction. We also emphasized the necessity of clear documentation and a well-defined scope statement to prevent misunderstandings and manage expectations effectively.

We further explored the creation of a Work Breakdown Structure (WBS) as a crucial tool for organizing project tasks and responsibilities. With detailed task breakdowns and effective use of technology, teams can enhance their efficiency and clarity. Last, we discussed strategies for validating and controlling scope, such as regular reviews, audits, and proactive communication with stakeholders. These practices help keep the project aligned with its goals and mitigate risks like scope creep, ensuring a smoother path to successful project completion.

Reference List

Atlassian. (2024). *Work Breakdown Structure in Project Management | The Workstream* . Atlassian. https://www.atlassian.com/work-management/project-management/work-breakdown-structure

Gibbons, S. (2022, October 23). *Stakeholder Interviews 101* . Nielsen Norman Group. https://www.nngroup.com/articles/stakeholder-interviews/

Landau, P. (2023, April 20). *Project scope statement: Include these 7 things* . ProjectManager.com. https://www.projectmanager.com/blog/project-scope-statement

Organ, C., & Bottorff, C. (2024, May 28). *Work breakdown structure as A project management tool* (R. Watts, Ed.). Forbes Advisor. https://www.forbes.com/advisor/business/what-is-work-breakdown-structure/

Scope and stakeholder management . (2019). Pmi.org. https://www.pmi.org/learning/library/stakeholder-management-pain-points-perils-prosperity-5955

Sandeep Kashyap. (2019, July 2). *Project Scope Management - Definition | Importance | Processes* . ProofHub. https://www.proofhub.com/articles/project-scope-management

Smith, L. W. (2020, September 7). *Stakeholder analysis* . Project Management Institute. https://www.pmi.org/learning/library/stakeholder-analysis-pivotal-practice-projects-8905

Welch, A. (2024). *Best practices for scope management guide* . *E-architect* . Retrieved from https://www.e-architect.com/articles/best-practices-for-scope-management

Chapter 4 - Time Management

Effective time management is essential for ensuring that projects stay on schedule and meet their deadlines. Without a systematic approach to planning, scheduling, and controlling project tasks, even the best-laid plans can go awry. Time management helps project managers organize activities, allocate resources wisely, and keep teams focused on priorities. By mastering the core components of time management, professionals can enhance their ability to deliver projects efficiently and meet stakeholder expectations. This chapter delves into practical methods that streamline task handling and promote a structured workflow, pivotal to any project's success.

In this chapter, you'll find detailed insights on how to define, sequence, and estimate project activities. We'll begin by discussing techniques for identifying and documenting all necessary tasks, ensuring clarity and accountability among team members. Following this, we'll explore effective sequencing strategies, highlighting the importance of understanding dependencies and using visual tools like network diagrams. You'll also learn about estimating activity durations accurately, leveraging expert judgment, historical data, and range estimation methods. Last, we'll cover ways to develop comprehensive schedules and implement control measures to track progress and make timely adjustments. By integrating these practices, you'll be well-equipped to manage project timelines effectively and navigate any challenges that arise along the way.

Defining Activities

Identifying and defining activities crucial for the successful execution of a project is fundamental to effective time management. This process provides clarity and direction, ensuring that all team members understand their roles and responsibilities. Here's how you can achieve this:

Activity List Creation

Creating a comprehensive list of activities is vital for project organization and clarity. A well-structured activity list guarantees that no critical tasks are overlooked. It also serves as the foundation for further planning and scheduling processes, reinforcing accountability among team members.

To begin with, brainstorm all potential activities required to complete the project. You can accomplish this through team meetings or by collecting individual input from team members. Next, group similar activities together to avoid being redundant and ensure comprehensive coverage of tasks. Each activity should have a clear description, making it easier to delegate responsibilities effectively.

For example, if you're managing a website development project, your activity list might include tasks like designing wireframes, coding the homepage, and testing usability. By listing out these activities, you can ensure that you account for each task, assign them appropriately, and track them throughout the project lifecycle.

Identifying and Analyzing Activities

Understanding each activity's purpose and its relation to project aims is critical. This process encourages deeper engagement with project goals and fosters ownership among team members. Aligning project activities with strategic objectives also promotes clarity in communication regarding roles and expectations.

Start by reviewing the project scope and objectives to identify key activities that align with strategic goals. Analyze how each activity contributes to these goals and whether they are necessary for project completion. Prioritize activities based on their importance and potential impact on the project's success.

For instance, in a marketing campaign project, identifying activities such as market research, content creation, and performance analysis helps ensure each step aligns with the overall campaign goals. This alignment not only enhances focus but also streamlines efforts toward achieving the desired outcomes.

Use of Templates

Leveraging templates to streamline the activity definition process can save time and ensure consistency across projects. Templates enhance accuracy and completeness by providing a guide during the listing phase, enabling quicker adaptation to similar projects in the future.

Using standardized templates allows project managers to maintain uniformity in activity lists, which are especially useful when managing multiple projects. Project managers can tailor templates to meet the specific requirements of each project, guaranteeing the inclusion of all relevant details.

For example, a template for a product launch project might include sections for market analysis, product development, marketing strategies, and post-launch evaluation. Project managers can ensure that all necessary activities are included by using this template, reducing the risk of missing critical tasks.

Documenting Activities

We cannot overstate the importance of thoroughly documenting each activity for clarity and guidance later on. Documentation serves as a reference point for future evaluations and audits, improves knowledge sharing within teams, supports compliance, and meets reporting requirements.

Each documented activity should include detailed descriptions, expected outcomes, resources required, and deadlines. Providing this level of detail gives team members a clear roadmap, ensuring that everyone understands what is expected and can work towards common goals.

For example, documenting an activity like "conducting user testing" in a software development project might include steps such as recruiting participants, preparing test scenarios, and analyzing feedback. This documentation not only guides the current project, but also serves as a valuable resource for future projects with similar requirements.

Sequencing Activities

Organizing project activities in a logical sequence is crucial for the efficient management and successful completion of any project. This involves understanding how tasks depend on one another, identifying dependencies, using visual tools like network diagrams, estimating leads and lags, and regularly reviewing sequences.

Dependency Identification

Understanding dependencies is crucial for accurate task sequencing. Dependencies are relationships between tasks that determine the order in which activities should occur. By identifying these relationships, you can visualize the project flow and optimize the schedule. For example, in a construction project, you must wait until the walls are built and inspected before beginning painting. Recognizing this dependency prevents potential bottlenecks and promotes effective resource allocation. Understanding dependencies helps project managers expect and mitigate risks, ensuring smoother project execution.

Use of Network Diagrams

Network diagrams are invaluable visual tools that simplify complex relationships among tasks. These diagrams make it easier to communicate project plans to stakeholders by illustrating how each task connects and influences others. Arrows in a network diagram represent tasks and their dependencies, helping identify the critical path—the series of dependent activities determining the shortest time required to complete a project (*Activity Sequencing and Network Diagrams | GEOG 871: Geospatial Technology Project Management*, n.d.).

The critical path method (CPM), a key feature of network diagrams, allows us to identify essential tasks that we must complete on time for the project to meet its deadline. Understanding the critical path enables better decision-making when dealing with changes or delays. If a task on the critical path is delayed, project managers can quickly assess its impact on the overall timeline and take corrective action to stay on track.

Estimating Leads and Lags

Leads and lags are adjustments introduced into activity sequencing to optimize schedules. A lead time allows a successor activity to start before its predecessor finishes. For example, in software development, the QA testing team might test before completing the entire coding phase. In contrast, lag time refers to a delay between two dependent tasks. For instance, after pouring concrete, you might need to wait a few days for it to cure before proceeding with construction.

Introducing leads and lags into the schedule without compromising quality ensures that projects maintain momentum and adapt to changing resource availability. This flexibility enhances stakeholder confidence as they see the project progressing efficiently (*What Is Lead Time and Lag Time in Project Management*, n.d.). It's important for project managers to review and adjust leads and lags continuously to align with the current project situation.

Conducting a Sequence Review

Regularly reviewing the activity sequence is vital for continuous improvement in project management practices. These reviews help identify potential adjustments needed as the project progresses, fostering an adaptive approach to managing tasks. Frequent reviews promote communication among team members, enabling them to identify challenges early and find solutions collaboratively. This proactive approach facilitates effective risk management by addressing issues before they escalate.

For instance, in a marketing campaign project, timely sequence reviews allow for reallocating tasks and resources to address changes in messaging based on initial feedback from a test audience, all while maintaining the project's timeline. Regularly updating the sequence based on real-time information keeps everyone aligned and informed, improving overall project efficiency.

Putting It All Together

To effectively manage project schedules, integrating dependency identification, network diagrams, estimating leads and lags, and conducting regular sequence reviews is essential. Project managers can ensure that projects meet their deadlines efficiently by understanding task dependencies, visualizing them through network diagrams, introducing flexible scheduling adjustments, and continually reviewing and refining the sequence.

Organizing activities in a logical sequence that reflects their dependencies not only optimizes the schedule but also enhances communication, resource allocation, and risk management. Projects proceed more smoothly when all team members understand how their work fits into the broader picture. This clarity fosters collaboration, improves morale, and ultimately leads to more successful project outcomes.

Understanding task dependencies is foundational to accurate sequencing. Identifying these relationships helps visualize the project flow, preventing disparities and optimizing the schedule. For instance, in software development, certain modules may need to be developed before integration testing. Properly identifying dependencies prevents potential bottlenecks and ensures efficient allocation of resources. By gaining a comprehensive understanding of dependencies, project managers can expect challenges and plan mitigation strategies accordingly.

Implementing network diagrams further simplifies complex task relationships. These visual tools provide a clear representation of the project's overall structure, making it easier to communicate plans to stakeholders. Each arrow and node in a network diagram illustrates task dependencies, facilitating better understanding and collaboration. Network diagrams aid in identifying the critical path — the sequence of dependent tasks that determine the minimum project duration (*Activity Sequencing and Network Diagrams | GEOG 871: Geospatial Technology Project Management*, n.d.). Highlighting the critical path allows project managers to focus on essential activities, ensuring timely delivery.

Incorporating leads and lags into activity sequencing provides additional flexibility. Leads enable a successor task to start before its predecessor finishes. For instance, content editing can begin while content creation is still underway. Lags introduce deliberate delays between tasks, such as permitting drying time for paint before applying a second coat. Strategic use of leads and lags optimizes schedules, maintaining progress despite changing conditions and enhancing stakeholder confidence (*What Is Lead Time and Lag Time in Project Management*, n.d.). Regular adjustments to leads and lags help align schedules with real-world circumstances, ensuring practicality without sacrificing quality.

Estimating Activity Durations

Estimating the duration of each activity is crucial for successful time management in project scheduling. By accurately forecasting how long tasks will take, we can ensure realistic schedules and efficient resource allocation.

Techniques for estimation provide flexibility based on project complexity. One popular method is expert judgment, where experienced professionals predict task durations based on their knowledge and experiences. This technique is useful for complex projects needing nuanced insights. (6 *Time Estimation Techniques: Pros + Cons–Blog*, 2021) Another common approach is analogous estimating, which involves comparing a current project with similar past projects to determine expected durations. While quicker, this method requires reliable historical data for accuracy.

Creating ranges for durations involves using three estimates: optimistic, pessimistic, and most likely. This method acknowledges uncertainty and prepares stakeholders for potential variations. For instance, if a task's optimistic duration is two days, a pessimistic is five, and most likely is three, these figures help manage expectations effectively. It enhances communication about possible timeline shifts, accommodating the inherent variability in project execution (Quizlet, n.d.).

When team members are engaged in the estimation process, they ensure diverse perspectives are considered, leading to more accurate predictions. When team members contribute to estimations, they bring unique insights from their specific areas of expertise. This inclusive approach builds a sense of ownership and responsibility among team members, enhancing their engagement and motivation.

Using historical data from previous projects significantly improves the precision of duration estimates. When historical performance data is accessible, it offers a benchmark for current project expectations. For example, if a prior project's similar task took four days on average, this information provides a realistic foundation for new estimates. This practice not only boosts forecasting accuracy but also fosters continuous improvement by learning from experiences.

Incorporating techniques for estimation ensures that project managers have the right tools for different scenarios. Expert judgment uses specialized knowledge, making it perfect for projects that lack detailed data but require professional analysis. Analogous estimating leverages similarities between projects, offering a speedy and cost-effective method to assess timelines. However, both methods need careful consideration to avoid biases and inaccuracies inherent in human judgment (Quizlet, n.d.).

Creating ranges for durations acknowledges the unpredictable nature of projects. The optimistic estimate reflects the best-case scenario, the pessimistic covers potential delays, and the most likely represents a realistic outcome. This method of estimating reduces the risk of being too optimistic about timelines and encourages proactive planning for uncertainties, aligning expectations with potential realities. For example, the formula for the expected duration $tE = \frac{tO + 4tM + tP}{6}$ balances these estimates, offering a well-rounded forecast.

By involving team members in the estimation process, project managers can access the collective intelligence of their teams. This collaborative effort not only refines estimates, but also strengthens commitment to the project's success. When individuals understand their role in achieving accurate estimates, they are more likely to commit to meeting deadlines, enhancing overall team cohesion and accountability.

Historical data utilization streamlines the estimation process through evidence-based benchmarks. Reviewing how previous similar tasks were performed helps us identify potential pitfalls and optimize current project plans. This approach shows alignment with the concept of continuous improvement, as it integrates lessons learned from experiences into future planning. By meticulously recording and analyzing historical data, we enable informed decision-making and set realistic expectations for stakeholders.

Techniques for estimation extend beyond merely assigning numbers to tasks; they underpin effective project management strategies. Accurate estimates allow for better scheduling, resource allocation, and risk management. Selecting the estimation method depends on the project's context, available data, and the precision level. Whether employing expert judgment for its nuanced insights or using analogous estimates for swift comparisons, each technique has distinct advantages suited to particular phases and types of projects.

Ranges in duration estimates further enhance a project manager's ability to navigate uncertainties. By preparing for varied outcomes, managers can develop contingency plans and communicate transparently with stakeholders. This preparedness builds confidence, as stakeholders appreciate the acknowledgment of potential deviations and the readiness to address them.

Engaging team members continues to play a vital role in refining estimates. Their hands-on experience and practical insights are invaluable in producing realistic timelines. Encouraging participation fosters a culture of shared responsibility, where each member contributes to the project's successful outcome. This collaborative environment boosts morale and drives the collective effort towards meeting project goals efficiently.

The strategic utilization of historical data represents another fundamental aspect of robust estimation practices. Historical insights provide concrete references, reducing guesswork and enhancing reliability. By systematically documenting and analyzing past performances, organizations build a repository of knowledge that informs future projects. This approach not only bolsters estimation accuracy, but also enhances organizational learning and continuous improvement.

Developing and Controlling Schedules

Creating a comprehensive project schedule and effectively implementing measures to control it throughout the project is vital for successful project management. Let's explore some key methodologies and strategies that can help achieve this goal.

First, understanding schedule development methods is crucial. Tools like Gantt charts and the Critical Path Method (CPM) are invaluable for this purpose. A Gantt chart provides a visual representation of the project timeline, breaking down all tasks and their durations. This allows project managers to see at a glance what needs to be done and when. By mapping out each task, Gantt charts help in prioritizing activities based on their critical nature, ensuring that the most essential tasks receive attention first. These charts reveal the resources needed at different stages of the project, aiding in resource allocation. This visualization facilitates efficient project execution, as teams are better equipped to expect and address potential bottlenecks.

The Critical Path Method focuses on identifying the longest stretch of dependent activities and measuring the time required to complete them from start to finish. Understanding the critical path helps in pinpointing activities that directly affect the overall project duration. By focusing on these tasks, project managers can prioritize resource allocation, proactively adjust timelines, and promptly address any delays in these critical tasks. Combining Gantt charts with CPM offers a robust approach to developing a project schedule that is both visually and analytically grounded.

Next, implementing schedule baselines is another essential aspect. Implementing schedule baselines is another essential aspect. A schedule baseline acts as an original approved version of the project schedule, which the team uses as a standard to measure project performance. Establishing a baseline early in the project lifecycle provides a reference point for evaluating progress against planned timelines. This helps in detecting variances between actual and planned progress, allowing for timely corrective actions. Communicating schedule baselines transparently ensures all stakeholders are aware of the initial plan and any subsequent changes, which fosters accountability and clarity. Once established, this baseline supports effective monitoring and control processes, enabling project managers to keep the project on track.

Monitoring techniques play a significant role in maintaining control over the project schedule. Continuous monitoring is essential for the prompt identification of delays or issues that need attention. Earned Value Management (EVM) is a widely used technique that offers valuable insights into project health. EVM integrates scope, schedule, and cost variables to provide a comprehensive view of project performance. By comparing planned vs. actual performance, EVM helps project managers determine whether the project is on track or if there are deviations that need intervention. For instance, if the earned value (work performed) is less than the planned value (work scheduled), it shows a delay, prompting project managers to investigate and resolve the underlying issues. Regular use of EVM and other monitoring techniques enables timely interventions, minimizing risks and keeping the project aligned with its goals.

To control changes effectively, a robust change control process is imperative. Changes are inevitable in any project, but uncontrolled changes can lead to scope creep, where the project's scope expands beyond its original objectives. A well-defined change control process ensures we document, evaluate, and approve all changes before implementing them. This process typically involves submitting a change request, assessing its impact on the project scope, schedule, and resources, and getting approval from relevant stakeholders. Documenting changes provides a simple trail of decision-making, making it easier to manage scope creep and maintain a focus on core deliverables. Emphasizing communication and stakeholder involvement throughout the change control process ensures everyone is aware of the changes and their implications, promoting transparency and trust.

Let's examine how we can apply these principles through a real-world example. Imagine a mid-level manager overseeing a software development project. The project involves multiple teams working on different modules that need to integrate seamlessly by the end date. First, the manager uses Gantt charts to develop a detailed schedule, outlining each team's tasks and deadlines. This visual aid helps identify the critical path, enabling the manager to focus on tasks that could delay the entire project if not completed on time. Next, the manager establishes a schedule baseline, sharing it with the teams and stakeholders to set clear expectations.

Throughout the project, continuous monitoring through Earned Value Management allows the manager to track progress accurately. When the manager detects a delay in one module, they swiftly re-allocates resources to address the issue, ensuring minimal impact on the overall timeline. Finally, as new requirements emerge, the manager employs a structured change control process to evaluate and approve necessary changes without disrupting the project flow. This approach ensures that the manager documents all modifications, understands their effects, and keeps the teams focused on delivering the core functionalities.

Final Thoughts

In this chapter, we've delved into the critical aspects of planning, scheduling, and controlling project activities to ensure timely completion. We've covered how to create and organize a detailed activity list, identify dependencies, use templates, and document every step thoroughly. These methods not only provide clarity and direction, but also enhance accountability and efficiency among team members. By aligning tasks with strategic objectives and employing tools like network diagrams and standardized documentation, project managers can foster a better understanding of individual roles and streamline the overall process.

It's essential to apply these principles consistently across all projects to maintain effective control over schedules. Embracing techniques such as regular sequence reviews and adjusting for leads and lags ensures that the project adapts to any changes smoothly. Engaging the team in these practices promotes a collaborative environment, thus enhancing morale and commitment. By implementing these strategies, you'll be well-equipped to navigate the complexities of project management, ensuring that your projects meet their deadlines and achieve desired outcomes efficiently.

Reference List

6 Time Estimation Techniques: Pros + Cons – blog . (2021, November). Actitime. https://www.actitime.com/project-time-estimation/project-estimation

Activity Sequencing and Network Diagrams | GEOG 871: Geospatial Technology Project Management . (n.d.). Www.e-Education.psu.edu. https://www.e-education.psu.edu/geog871/l5_p4.html

Brown, L. (2021, June 3). *Defining Activity List and Examples For a Project* . Invensis Learning Blog. https://www.invensislearning.com/blog/define-activity-list-in-a-project/

Guthrie, G. (2022, November 18). *How to define project activities and milestones as a project manager* . Nulab. https://nulab.com/learn/project-management/project-activities-and-milestones-in-project-management/

Quizlet. (n.d.). *Estimate activity duration tools and techniques flashcards* . Retrieved from https://quizlet.com/492409749/estimate-activity-duration-tools-and-techniques-flash-cards/

What is lead time and lag time in project management . (n.d.). Www.hellobonsai.com. https://www.hellobonsai.com/blog/lag-time-and-lead-time-in-project-management

Chapter 5 - Cost Management

Cost management plays a vital role in ensuring the financial efficiency of projects. Meticulous planning and controlling costs in cost management ensure that we allocate resources wisely and keep expenditures within the budget. Project managers use a well-developed cost management plan as a roadmap, outlining how they will estimate costs, determine budgets, and control expenses throughout the project lifecycle. By adhering to these guidelines, project teams can navigate the financial complexities of any project with greater confidence and precision.

In this chapter, we delve into the essential components of cost management, beginning with the process of estimating project costs. Readers will gain insight into various estimation techniques, such as analogous, parametric, and bottom-up estimation, and learn how to leverage historical data and expert insights to enhance accuracy. The chapter then explores the creation of a comprehensive budget, emphasizing the importance of cost aggregation and the use of specialized tools and techniques for efficient budgeting. Finally, we discuss the critical aspects of cost control, including performance measurement techniques like Earned Value Management (EVM), variance analysis, and effective reporting and communication strategies. Through these discussions, readers will gain the knowledge and skills to effectively manage project costs, ensuring successful project outcomes.

Planning Cost Management

In the realm of project management, a well-structured cost management plan serves as a fundamental tool for ensuring financial efficiency throughout a project's lifecycle. It is impossible to overstate the importance of such a plan, as it offers clear guidelines for estimating costs, determining budgets, and controlling expenses, all of which are crucial for successfully completing any project.

A comprehensive cost management plan begins with understanding its core components. This plan lays the foundation for managing the budget, from initial estimation to final reporting. The plan sets forth the methodologies for cost estimation, identifies necessary resources, and outlines how to control and monitor those costs. By defining these elements up front, project managers can create a roadmap that aligns with both the project's objectives and financial constraints.

At the heart of an effective cost management plan is estimating costs. This involves predicting the financial resources required for each phase of the project. Estimating costs accurately requires a detailed analysis of all project activities, materials, and labor needs. This not only helps in avoiding budget overruns but also allows for the identification of potential cost-saving opportunities. According to research, inaccurate cost estimation and improper resource allocation pose a heightened risk of exceeding the budget, which can lead to project failure (*What Is a Cost Management Plan in Project Management?*, n.d.).

Once we estimate the costs, the next step is to create a budget. This budget should reflect the total expected costs of the project, broken down into manageable components. A well-defined budget serves as a financial blueprint, guiding the allocation of resources and helping to keep expenses under control. It is essential that the budget remains flexible to accommodate any changes or unforeseen circumstances that may arise during the project. Using tools like Gantt charts can aid in visually separating the budget into stages, making it easier to manage and adjust as needed.

An integral part of cost management is the involvement of stakeholders. Stakeholders, who may include clients, team members, and investors, play a critical role in shaping the financial landscape of the project. When developing the cost management plan, it is important to consider the expectations and input of stakeholders. When developing the cost management plan, it is important to consider the expectations and input of clients, team members, and investors, as they play a critical role in shaping the financial landscape of the project. This alignment ensures that the project's financial plans meet the expectations of all parties involved, minimizing conflicts and facilitating smoother project execution.

Aligning the cost management plan with the overall project goals is another key aspect. It is important for the plan to align with the project's strategic objectives and ensure that financial resources are allocated to high-priority areas. This alignment guarantees that the budget reflects the most critical aspects of the project, which are indispensable for its success. By prioritizing spending on essential activities, project managers can optimize resource utilization and enhance the chances of delivering the project on time and within budget.

Defining the processes within a cost management plan provides clarity and direction. These processes typically include cost estimation, budgeting, and cost control. Each process has specific steps and guidelines that help project managers navigate the financial complexities of the project. For instance, cost control measures involve regular monitoring and tracking of expenditures against the budget. Techniques such as Earned Value Management (EVM) can assess performance and identify variances that may require corrective action. Clear processes not only streamline budgeting activities but also facilitate more accurate forecasting and better decision-making.

Another important element to consider is the establishment of control thresholds. These thresholds act as triggers for taking corrective action if the project deviates from its financial plan. For example, setting a threshold at a certain percentage of budget overrun can prompt a review of expenses and implementation of cost-saving measures. Control thresholds proactively address financial issues, reducing the risk of significant budget breaches.

The cost management plan should outline the reporting formats and frequency. Regular reports on financial status, including budget updates and expenditure summaries, keep all stakeholders informed about the project's progress and any financial concerns. Transparency in reporting builds trust and enables timely interventions if needed. Consistent communication through well-structured reports helps maintain fiscal discipline and supports informed decision-making.

The goal of a cost management plan is to ensure that projects execute efficiently, optimally using financial resources. Proper cost planning enables project managers to expect future expenses, allocate funds wisely, and avoid unnecessary costs. This proactive approach not only enhances financial stability but also contributes to the overall success of the project. Effective cost management practices help in tracking project progress, managing bottlenecks promptly, and preventing scope creep by maintaining transparency between relevant parties (*What Is Project Cost Management? (Importance, Steps, & Benefits)*, n.d.).

Estimating Costs

Cost management is a critical aspect of project management, and accurately estimating project costs is fundamental to financial efficiency. This sub-point aims to equip readers with techniques and tools for accurate cost estimation based on comprehensive analysis.

Understanding various estimation techniques is crucial for flexibility in forecasting. Analogous estimation leverages data from past projects that are like predict the costs of the current project. This method is straightforward and quick, ideal for early project phases or when limited information is available. However, its accuracy depends heavily on the similarity between the projects being compared. Multiple reference projects should increase reliability and minimize subjectivity.

Parametric estimation uses statistical relationships between historical data, and other variables to determine cost estimates. For example, in construction, parameters like square footage can help predict costs. Although this technique is less common in IT because of inefficiencies in using parameters like code lines, it can still be useful in fields where quantifiable metrics are available. Encouraging regular updates and maintaining a robust database ensures data quality and completeness.

Bottom-up estimation involves breaking down the project into smaller components and estimating costs for each part individually before aggregating them. This method provides a detailed breakdown, resulting in high accuracy. It requires significant time and effort, but provides precise estimates that help in managing resources effectively.

Using historical data is another vital strategy for improving estimate accuracy. Historical data serves as a benchmark, which allows project managers to base their predictions on actual past performance. This not only improves accuracy but also helps in identifying trends and patterns that can inform future projects. To harness the full potential of historical data, maintaining comprehensive records and regularly updating them is essential. Analyzing past projects' successes and failures enables project managers to replicate best practices and avoid previous mistakes.

Engaging Subject Matter Experts (SMEs) adds another layer of precision to cost estimation. SMEs possess specialized knowledge that can lead to more accurate estimates. Their insights help uncover potential issues and opportunities that might not be clear through data analysis alone. Selecting the right experts is key. Look for professionals with proven experience and knowledge in the relevant domain. It's also important to ensure that professionals with proven experience and knowledge in the relevant domain have accurate past predictions, and this can be done by maintaining a performance database. Expert judgment brings depth of insight, providing quicker and flexible estimations. However, biases and subjectivity can affect outcomes. Using structured techniques like Poker Planning or the Delphi method can minimize bias. A diverse panel of experts ensures balanced perspectives. Establishing a network of experts and maintaining good relationships to ensure their availability when needed can mitigate challenges related to expert accessibility. Remote consultation options could widen the pool of experts.

Factoring in contingencies is an essential practice in cost estimation. Contingency planning offers a buffer against unforeseen costs that may arise during the project lifecycle. Projects frequently encounter challenges, like changes in scope, limited resources, and external influences. Adding a contingency reserve helps manage these risks effectively without derailing the budget. The amount set aside for contingencies should be based on the project's complexity, potential risks identified during the planning phase, and historical data. Regularly reviewing and adjusting the contingency reserve throughout the project ensures it remains adequate to cover unexpected expenses.

While detailed analysis and precise techniques form the backbone of cost estimation, it's equally important to communicate these estimates effectively to stakeholders. Clear communication builds trust and ensures all parties understand the rationale behind the numbers. Using visual aids like charts and graphs can make complex data more accessible. Regular status updates keep everyone informed about any changes in cost estimates and the reasons behind them. Engaging stakeholders in the estimation process fosters collaboration and agreement, reducing the likelihood of disputes later on.

Determining Budget

Creating an effective project budget is key to successful cost management in any project. To achieve this, thorough planning is essential. This section provides a step-by-step guide, explores the concept of cost aggregation, and highlights essential tools and techniques for budgeting. We will also emphasize the importance of monitoring the budget against actual expenditures to manage variances effectively.

Steps for Budget Development

Developing a project budget begins with outlining the project's scope and identifying all tasks and deliverables. Start by defining the activities required to complete the project.

From these activities, you can derive their associated costs, including labor, materials, equipment, and any other expenses.

1. **Define Project Scope:** Clearly outline what the project aims to achieve and its boundaries. This helps prevent scope creep, which can lead to unforeseen costs.

2. **Breaking Down Activities:** Divide the project into smaller tasks and work packages. The team should detail each task enough to assign costs accurately.

3. **Estimate Costs:** Use historical data, expert judgment, and standardized cost estimating techniques to predict the expenses associated with each task. Techniques like analogous estimation, parametric modeling, and bottom-up estimation can be useful here.

4. **Consolidate Estimates:** Summarize the estimated costs of all tasks to get a total project budget. Include all indirect costs, such as overheads and administrative expenses.

5. **Review and Refine:** Involve stakeholders in reviewing the budget estimates to ensure nothing is overlooked. Their insights could highlight additional costs not initially considered (Involvement of Stakeholders).

6. **Get Approval:** Present the final budget to project sponsors or financial managers for approval. Before, make sure you secure all necessary authorizations.

Cost Aggregation

Cost aggregation is summing up individual costs to form a total project cost estimate. Project managers can pinpoint significant cost drivers and identify areas where savings can be achieved by identifying and grouping costs.

1. **Identify Major Cost Drivers:** Determine which elements of the project contribute most to the overall cost. Typically, labor, materials, and equipment are primary cost drivers in projects.

2. **Group Similar Costs:** Aggregate costs by category in order to simplify analysis. For example, group all labor costs together and all material costs together, etc.

3. **Analyze Potential Savings:** Examine grouped costs to identify opportunities for cost-saving strategies. Bulk purchasing, negotiating better rates, or optimizing resource use can contribute to reduced expenses.

4. **Create a Cost Baseline:** Establish a baseline against which actual costs can be measured. This helps track financial performance over the project lifecycle.

Tools and Techniques for Budgeting

Using specialized tools and methodologies enhances the accuracy and efficiency of budget creation. Several tools and techniques can streamline the budgeting process:

1. **Project Management Software:** Tools like Microsoft Project, Asana, or Trello offer features for tracking

expenses, resource allocation, and budget forecasting. These tools help visualize the budget flow and facilitate real-time adjustments.

2. **Spreadsheets:** While basic, spreadsheets can be very effective for smaller projects. They allow for detailed breakdowns and easy modifications, but require manual updates.

3. **Earned Value Management (EVM):** This technique integrates project scope, schedule, and cost variables to assess project performance and progress. EVM metrics, like the Cost Performance Index (CPI) and Schedule Performance Index (SPI), provide valuable insights into the financial health.

4. **Cost Estimating Software:** Tools like RSMeans, Clear Estimates, and CostX specifically designed to generate precise cost estimates based on industry standards and historical data.

5. **Resource Allocation Models:** These models help in distributing resources efficiently across various tasks, ensuring optimal use without overspending.

Monitoring Budget vs. Actuals

Regularly comparing the budget to actual expenditures is crucial in managing project finances. This practice helps in early identification of variances, allowing for timely corrective measures.

1. **Track Expenses:** Maintain a detailed record of all expenditures. Ensure that you accurately document and regularly update receipts, invoices, and financial statements.

2. **Regular Audits:** Conduct periodic audits to compare planned versus actual spending. Identify discrepancies and analyze their causes.

3. **Variance Analysis:** Assess the financial impact of any variances. Positive variances show cost savings, while negative variances highlight overspending that needs addressing.

4. **Corrective Actions** : Implement strategies to manage cost overruns. This might involve reallocating resources, cutting non-essential expenses, or revising project plans.

5. **Update Stakeholders:** Keep all relevant parties informed about the project's financial status. Transparent communication fosters trust and enables collaborative problem-solving.

Controlling Costs

Establishing Cost Control Measures

One of the fundamental strategies to keep your project within budget is establishing effective cost control measures.

Regular updates and evaluations are pivotal in helping project managers navigate financial challenges. This begins with a detailed baseline budget that includes all expected expenses, serving as a reference point throughout the project lifecycle. Continuous monitoring of this baseline allows for the identification of any deviations from the planned budget early on.

Setting up periodic reviews helps in assessing the project's financial health. For instance, weekly or monthly financial reports can provide insights into expenditure patterns, making it easier to spot areas where costs are spiraling out of control. Adopting software tools that automate these updates ensures accuracy and saves time, enabling project managers to focus on addressing financial discrepancies swiftly.

Implementing corrective actions is another crucial aspect of cost control measures. When identifying variances, it's crucial to investigate their root causes and promptly implement solutions. This may involve reallocating resources, negotiating with suppliers for better rates, or cutting down on non-essential expenditures. It's also beneficial to involve your team in these evaluations, since they might offer practical solutions based on their day-to-day operations experience.

Performance Measurement Techniques

To gain deeper insights into whether your project is progressing as financially planned, performance measurement techniques like Earned Value Management (EVM) play a critical role. EVM integrates cost, schedule, and scope to assess project performance comprehensively. Understanding its key metrics—Planned Value (PV), Actual Cost (AC), and Earned Value (EV)—is essential for interpreting data accurately.

Planned Value (PV) represents the budgeted amount allotted for work scheduled up to a certain date. It acts as a benchmark against which actual performance is measured. Actual Cost (AC) shows the total expenditure incurred for the work completed by that date. Earned Value (EV) reflects the approved budget for the work actually performed. Comparing these metrics helps identify Cost Variance (CV) and Schedule Variance (SV), providing a sign of how well the project adheres to the financial plan.

For instance, a positive CV means your project is under budget, while a negative CV shows over-budgeting issues. Similarly, calculating the Cost Performance Index (CPI) allows you to understand cost efficiency. A CPI greater than one signifies cost-effective performance, whereas a CPI less than one suggests budget overruns. By regularly applying EVM, project managers can make informed decisions about resource allocation and take corrective actions before minor issues escalate.

Variance Analysis

Variance analysis is integral to identifying deviations from the planned budget and understanding their implications. At its core, variance analysis involves comparing the actual performance data against the baseline budget to recognize spending patterns and potential problems early. Managers need to categorize variances into positive and negative variances, each requiring different management strategies.

Positive variances show underspending, potentially signaling opportunities to reallocate resources to other critical areas requiring additional funding. On the other hand, negative variances flag overspending, emphasizing the need for immediate corrective measures to prevent any further budget deviations. Conducting variance analysis routinely enhances visibility in project performance and supports improved decision-making through real-time data.

However, accurate variance analysis relies heavily on precise and timely data collection. Inaccurate data can lead to misguided conclusions and ineffective actions. Thus, fostering a culture of meticulous data management is essential. Regular training on data collection methods and ensuring consistency in reporting standards can mitigate inaccuracies and improve the overall reliability of variance analysis.

Reporting and Communication

Effective reporting and communication are indispensable for maintaining transparency and keeping all stakeholders informed about the project's financial status. Timely, detailed reports provide a clear view of financial progress and highlight any issues that may require attention. These reports should include critical metrics, such as actual costs, budget forecasts, and variances, presented in an understandable format for all stakeholders, regardless of their financial expertise.

Regularly scheduled meetings to discuss these reports foster open communication and collaborative problem-solving. Stakeholders can provide valuable feedback, suggest improvements, and support necessary changes. By utilizing project management software with reporting capabilities, you can streamline this process and guarantee that reports are automatically generated and distributed to relevant parties.

Transparency in financial reporting also builds trust among stakeholders. When everyone involved has access to the same financial data, it simplifies the alignment of project goals with budget constraints. Open communication channels also ensure that stakeholders promptly address any concerns or suggestions, preventing misunderstandings and promoting a collaborative approach to financial management.

Including these practices in your project management routine establishes a strong foundation for effective cost control. Establishing cost control measures, employing performance measurement techniques like EVM, conducting thorough variance analysis, and maintaining transparent reporting and communication collectively contribute to keeping your project within budget and ensuring financial efficiency.

Final Thoughts

In this chapter, we delved into the essentials of cost management in project management. We covered the importance of creating a thorough cost management plan that includes accurate cost estimation, budgeting, and the involvement of stakeholders. These elements form the backbone for managing financial resources effectively, ensuring that projects run smoothly and stay within budget. Understanding techniques like analogous estimation, parametric estimation, and bottom-up estimation can help predict costs accurately. Engaging Subject Matter Experts and factoring in contingencies can significantly improve estimate precision.

We also explored how to structure a robust budget and highlighted tools and methodologies to aid in budgeting. From employing software solutions to using Earned Value Management for performance tracking, each method contributes to effective budget monitoring. By establishing control thresholds and regularly analyzing variances, we ensure that we quickly address any financial hiccups. Transparent communication and detailed reporting keep all stakeholders informed and aligned with the project's financial goals. By adopting these practices, project managers can navigate the complexities of cost management and steer their projects toward success.

Reference List

Asana. (2022, October 1). *Cost Control: How to Monitor Project Spending to Increase Profitability • Asana* . Asana. https://asana.com/resources/cost-control

How to Estimate Project: Time, Cost and Resources . (n.d.). Planyway.com. https://planyway.com/blog/project-estimation

Home - Haz Financial Advisors . (2024, April). HAZ ADVISORS LLC. https://hazadvisors.com/cost-estimation/

Landau, P. (2023, March 1). *Resource Management - A Quick Guide* . ProjectManager.com. https://www.projectmanager.com/blog/quick-guide-resource-management

Martins, J. (2022, December 5). *Resource Allocation Tips for Project Managers • Asana* . Asana. https://asana.com/resources/resource-allocation

What is Variance Analysis? Earned Value Management explained. (n.d.). Www.gatherinsights.com. https://www.gatherinsights.com/en/glossary/earned-value-defintions/variance-analysis

What Is Project Cost Management? (Importance, Steps, & Benefits) . (n.d.). Www.usemotion.com. https://www.usemotion.com/blog/project-cost-management

What is a Cost Management Plan in Project Management? (n.d.). Wrike. https://www.wrike.com/project-management-guide/faq/what-is-cost-management-plan/

Chapter 6 - Quality Management

Managing quality is essential for any project to succeed. By prioritizing quality management, you guarantee that all project deliverables meet the required standards and fulfill stakeholder expectations. This chapter dives into the nitty-gritty of creating a structured approach to quality by establishing a quality management plan (QMP). Through this plan, you'll learn how to align your project's ambitions with what stakeholders expect, paving a clear way for consistent and high-quality execution.

In this chapter, we'll explore how to develop the components of an effective QMP meticulously. You'll discover how to set specific metrics, define quality objectives, and assign responsibilities to your team. We'll also cover practical steps to integrate the QMP seamlessly into your overall project plan, ensuring every phase of planning to execution meets predefined quality standards. You'll learn the importance of engaging stakeholders in the planning process, which not only enriches the quality measures but also ensures they are both realistic and relevant. By the end of this chapter, you'll have a robust framework for maintaining quality throughout your project's lifecycle.

Planning Quality Management

Establishing a quality management plan (QMP) is essential for maintaining quality throughout the project lifecycle. By creating a structured approach to quality, you align your project's objectives with stakeholder expectations and set a clear path for consistent execution.

Developing a QMP starts by ensuring that the plan is in harmony with the project's goals and stakeholder requirements. This alignment acts as a guiding framework for the entire project, ensuring that every step taken contributes to achieving these predefined objectives. For instance, if the project aims to deliver a software product, the QMP will outline steps to ensure the software meets specified performance benchmarks and user needs.

One of the critical components of a QMP is defining specific metrics. Quantifiable measures define specific metrics that provide a clear standard against which the project's quality can be assessed. Metrics, such as defect rates, code quality standards, or customer satisfaction scores, help in evaluating whether the project is on track. Early identification of any deviations through this metrics allows for prompt corrective actions, thus maintaining the overall quality. For instance, if a project's metric shows a high number of defects in the initial testing phase, immediate attention can address these issues before they escalate further.

Proactively identifying risks that might affect quality and establishing mitigation strategies is another foundational aspect of a robust QMP. Risks could range from technical challenges to resource limitations or external factors as market changes. By anticipating these risks early on, project managers can devise strategies to prevent them from affecting quality. For example, if there's a risk of insufficient testing because of tight timelines, the plan might include additional resources or automated testing tools to ensure thorough quality checks.

Engaging stakeholders in the quality planning process is crucial for ensuring that the quality measures align with actual needs and fostering a collaborative environment. Stakeholders, including clients, end-users, and team members, provide diverse perspectives and insights that enrich the quality management process. Their involvement ensures that the quality criteria are realistic and relevant. For instance, involving end-users in setting usability standards can lead to a more user-friendly final product.

To develop an effective QMP, follow these guidelines:

1. **Identify Quality Requirements:** Understand what quality means for the project by consulting with stakeholders to capture their expectations and requirements. This helps in setting clear and achievable quality goals.

1. **Select Appropriate Standards:** Choose relevant industry standards, best practices, and guidelines that align with the project's objectives. Adhering to these standards provides a benchmark for quality and ensures compliance with regulatory requirements.

1. **Establish Quality Objectives:** Set clear, measurable goals that align with the overall project purpose. These

objectives should be Specific, Measurable, Achievable, Relevant, and Time-bound (SMART).

1. **Assign Responsibilities:** Clearly define roles and responsibilities for quality-related tasks among the members of the project team. Everyone involved should know their duties and how they contribute to maintaining quality.

1. **Plan Quality Assurance and Control Activities:** Develop a detailed plan outlining quality assurance (QA) and quality control (QC) activities. QA focuses on preventive measures to ensure processes are efficient, while QC involves inspecting and testing deliverables to identify flaws.

1. **Define Metrics:** Identify key performance indicators (KPIs) and other metrics to assess the project's quality at various stages. Metrics provide a basis for evaluating progress and identifying areas needing improvement.

1. **Integrate with the Project Plan:** Ensure the QMP is seamlessly incorporated into the overall project plan. Coordination with other project management processes is vital for cohesion.

1. **Communicate and Train:** Make sure all team members understand the QMP, its objectives, and their roles in implementing it. Providing training sessions can enhance understanding and commitment to quality standards.

Performing Quality Assurance

To meet stakeholders' expectations and successfully deliver project outcomes, project teams must ensure that they follow and maintain quality standards during the execution of the project. Regular quality audits play a pivotal role in this process, offering an objective evaluation of the adherence to defined quality standards. These audits help identify any deviations from the planned objectives, offering a clear picture of the areas where improvements are needed. For example, if a software development project deviates from coding standards, a quality audit can pinpoint these discrepancies early on, allowing for prompt corrective actions. This proactive approach not only rectifies issues but also fortifies the overall quality management framework by promoting continuous improvement, thus fostering a culture where high-quality outputs are the norm.

Implementing process improvement techniques, such as Lean and Six Sigma further strengthens quality management by emphasizing efficiency and reducing defects. Lean method emphasizes eliminating waste within processes, streamlining operations and maximizing value for the customer. Six Sigma aims to minimize variability and defects by using statistical analysis. Combining these methodologies into Lean Six Sigma creates a powerful tool for enhancing operational efficiency. For instance, in a manufacturing setting, employing Lean Six Sigma can lead to significant reductions in production cycle times and defects, improving product quality and customer satisfaction (GoLeanSixSigma.com, 2019). This systematic approach ensures that every step of the process builds quality instead of relying on inspection at the end.

Effective training is another cornerstone for ensuring quality standards throughout a project's lifecycle. Training programs should equip team members with the essential skills and knowledge to meet established quality expectations. For example, training sessions on the latest quality control tools and techniques can empower employees to perform their roles more effectively. When team members understand how to use tools, such as control charts or statistical process control, they are better positioned to identify potential quality issues before they escalate. Continuous training ensures that everyone stays informed about the latest industry advancements and follows the best methods, resulting in consistently excellent results. Investing in training not only enhances individual competencies, but also improves the collective performance of the project team.

Regular quality reviews at key milestones act as critical checkpoints to ensure that the project stays aligned with its quality objectives. These reviews provide an opportunity for timely intervention, enabling the project team to address any emerging issues before they become significant problems. For example, in a construction project, conducting quality reviews after each major phase, such as foundation pouring or framing, helps ensure each segment meets the specified standards. This practice fosters a sense of shared responsibility towards quality among team members, encouraging collaborative efforts to maintain high standards. Quality reviews also facilitate open communication between different stakeholders, promoting transparency and accountability throughout the project. The regularity of these reviews ensures that quality remains a central focus, ultimately leading to superior project outcomes.

Conducting regular quality audits is essential for maintaining high standards. These audits reveal inconsistencies and areas needing enhancement. For example, in the food industry, HACCP systems identify potential food safety hazards and enforce strict hygiene practices and temperature monitoring (Team, 2024). Similarly, in the software industry, thorough testing at various development stages helps catch and fix bugs early. Audits not only identify issues but also validate that the implemented quality measures are effective. Involving external auditors can bring fresh perspectives and expert advice, further strengthening the quality management system.

Implementing process improvement techniques, such as Lean and Six Sigma systematically removes inefficiencies and defects. Lean focuses on reducing waste in all forms, while Six Sigma uses data-driven methods to achieve near-perfect quality levels. For example, Lean techniques can streamline supply chain processes, reducing delays and costs. Six Sigma's DMAIC framework (Define, Measure, Analyze, Improve, Control) provides a structured approach to problem-solving. By integrating these methodologies, organizations can achieve a balanced approach to efficiency and quality, leading to higher customer satisfaction and competitive advantage.

Effective training equips team members with the skills to meet quality standards consistently. Training should cover both technical aspects and quality management principles. For example, training on statistical process control can help team members understand and monitor process variability, making it easier to maintain quality. Ongoing professional development ensures that the team stays current with industry advancements. Fostering a culture of continuous learning encourages team members to implement improvements actively, enhancing overall project quality.

Regular quality reviews at key milestones provide opportunities for timely interventions and reinforce a culture of quality. These reviews assess whether the project is on track to meet its quality objectives and allow for adjustments as needed. For example, in the construction industry, project managers conduct quality reviews after each major milestone, such as electrical and plumbing installations, to ensure compliance with safety codes and design specifications. Such reviews encourage collaboration among team members, as everyone has a stake in the project's success. They also offer a platform for recognizing good practices and addressing concerns, promoting a proactive approach to quality management.

Controlling Quality

Monitoring and measuring project quality is a vital practice to ensure that deliverables meet the defined standards. This process entails a range of strategic approaches and tools designed to evaluate and maintain the desired level of quality throughout the project's lifecycle.

One essential tool in quality control is the use of control charts. These charts serve as a visual representation of project performance over time, enabling project managers to monitor various metrics continuously. By plotting data points within predetermined control limits, project managers can quickly identify and address deviations from the set standards. For instance, if a construction project consistently records delays beyond the acceptable threshold on a control chart, it signals an immediate need for investigation and corrective action. By using such tools, one can maintain a steady quality flow and ensure early detection and efficient management of any variations. A guideline here is to update control charts regularly with current data to reflect accurate project performance.

Analyzing performance data against predefined metrics is another crucial aspect of maintaining project quality. Predefined metrics, such as key performance indicators (KPIs), provide quantifiable measures to assess the extent to which project objectives are being met. For example, in a software development project, the team can track bug frequency rates, user acceptance test results, and system uptime against benchmarks to gauge performance. Data analysis enables project managers to make informed, data-driven decisions about necessary adjustments to meet quality targets. This analytical approach ensures that quality management is not based on assumptions but on hard evidence, facilitating more precise planning and execution. It's important to establish these metrics at the project's outset to serve as a clear benchmark for ongoing evaluations.

Effective change management is also pivotal in monitoring and measuring project quality. Any project inevitably involves change, and effectively managing these changes can have a significant impact on overall quality. Implementing robust change management processes ensures modifications do not detract from the project's quality standards. For example, when altering the design specifications of a new product, a structured change management process will include thorough impact assessments and reviews from quality assurance teams. This ensures that the final products remain reliable while allowing for necessary changes. According to research, measuring compliance with changes and overall performance shows a strong correlation with meeting or exceeding project objectives (Horlick, 2024). Therefore, it is crucial to establish clear guidelines for handling changes, making sure they align with quality benchmarks.

Continuous feedback loops from stakeholders play a critical role in ensuring developing quality standards and fostering accountability. Regular feedback sessions engage stakeholders and continually align their expectations and requirements with what the project delivers. For example, in a customer service improvement project, collecting frequent feedback from both customers and front-line staff can highlight areas needing enhancement. This stakeholder involvement not only keeps the project on track concerning quality standards but also promotes a sense of ownership and accountability among all parties involved. Importantly, these feedback mechanisms should be systematic and consistent, providing timely and actionable insights into the project's quality performance (Karpenkova, 2023).

To implement these strategies effectively, there are several practical steps that can guide project managers and their teams. For quality control measures like control charts, it's advisable to follow these steps: first, identify relevant metrics that reflect critical quality attributes; second, establish control limits based on historical data or industry standards; third, collect and chart data consistently; and finally, analyze the charts regularly to identify trends or deviations. This approach ensures that the project stays within defined quality boundaries.

For performance measurement, establishing clear and specific KPIs is essential. Start by defining measurable outcomes that align with project goals. For example, setting a target for defect reduction in a manufacturing process might include specific KPIs, like the number of defects per thousand units produced. Regularly review these KPIs against actual performance data, using statistical analysis tools to gain deeper insights. Review and update the metrics periodically to keep them relevant throughout the project's duration.

In managing change effectively, developing a detailed change management plan is beneficial. This plan should include processes for submitting change requests, evaluating their impact on quality, and getting necessary approvals. Developing a detailed change management plan can help ensure that everyone is aligned and understands their roles in preserving quality during changes, and regular training sessions can help achieve this.

Finally, to establish continuous feedback loops, create structured channels for receiving feedback, such as surveys, focus groups, or regular review meetings. Establish a feedback schedule and make it a routine part of the project's lifecycle. Analyze the feedback to derive actionable insights and communicate the findings and subsequent actions back to stakeholders. This transparency builds trust and reinforces commitment to maintaining high-quality standards.

Quality Improvement Tools

Facilitating continuous quality improvement throughout a project is essential to ensure that all deliverables consistently meet or exceed quality standards. Effective quality management processes help identify and address underlying issues, thus preventing their recurrence.

Root cause analysis techniques are crucial for identifying the root causes of quality issues. One such technique is the Fishbone diagram, also known as the Ishikawa or cause-and-effect diagram. This visual tool helps teams organize potential causes of a problem into categories like people, machines, materials, methods, and the environment. By systematically evaluating each category, teams can better understand how different factors contribute to quality problems and prioritize which issues need immediate attention. For instance, if a project consistently faces delays, the Fishbone diagram might reveal that the root cause is inadequate training for team members rather than a lack of resources. Addressing this root cause prevents similar issues from recurring and contributes to overall project success.

Another effective method for continuous quality improvement is the PDCA (Plan-Do-Check-Act) cycle. The PDCA cycle offers a structured framework for iterative learning and quality enhancement. The first step, Plan, involves identifying a specific problem or area for improvement and devising a strategy to address it. For example, if customer feedback shows dissatisfaction with product features, the planning phase would involve gathering data, setting objectives, and developing an action plan to enhance those features.

The next phase, Do, entails executing the plan on a small scale to test its effectiveness. This might involve piloting a new process or implementing a minor change in the current workflow. During this phase, teams must meticulously document their actions and collect data to measure outcomes.

In the Check phase, teams evaluate the results of the test implementation against the performance metrics established during the planning phase. If the changes yield positive results, the teams proceed to the final Act phase, where they standardize and integrate successful strategies into regular operations. Continuous cycles of PDCA enable organizations to ensure sustained quality improvements over time by systematically refining processes (Peterka, 2024).

Statistical quality control tools play a vital role in monitoring and improving process variability. Tools like control charts and histograms help project managers visualize data trends, identify variations, and make data-driven decisions. For instance, a control chart can highlight fluctuations in product quality over time, enabling managers to investigate and rectify deviations before they escalate into major issues. By analyzing this data, teams can pinpoint specific stages in the production process that require change, reducing defects and enhancing overall quality.

Control charts distinguish between common cause variation, which is inherent to the process, and special cause variation, which stems from specific, identifiable events. Understanding these variations helps teams determine whether process adjustments or fundamental redesigns are necessary. For example, if a control chart reveals a spike in defects because of a machinery malfunction, resolving this issue can quickly restore consistent quality levels.

Benchmarking is another valuable technique for facilitating continuous quality improvement. By comparing project performance against industry standards and best practices, organizations can identify areas needing improvement and maintain a competitive edge. Benchmarking involves analyzing key performance indicators (KPIs), such as cycle time, defect rates, and customer satisfaction scores. These comparisons provide insights into how other organizations achieve high-quality standards and offer actionable strategies for enhancing one's own processes.

For example, a software development firm might benchmark its bug resolution time against that of industry leaders. If the industry standard is to resolve bugs within 24 hours while the firm's average is 48 hours, this discrepancy highlights an area for improvement. Implementing best practices observed in top-performing companies, such as automated testing and more efficient workflows, can help bridge this gap and elevate the firm's quality standards.

Implementing these quality improvement methodologies requires a data-driven approach. Continuous collection and analysis of relevant data enable teams to identify inefficiencies and focus improvement efforts where they are most needed. Data serves as the foundation for informed decision-making, guiding teams toward effective strategies that enhance quality and meet customer expectations.

Engaging stakeholders in the quality improvement process is also crucial. Collaboration and consensus-building promote a shared sense of responsibility and commitment to achieving high-quality objectives. Regular communication and feedback loops ensure that stakeholder expectations align with project objectives, fostering a collaborative environment that values continuous improvement.

Organizations should cultivate a culture of continuous improvement by encouraging team members at all levels to contribute ideas and take part in quality enhancement initiatives. Techniques like brainstorming sessions, mind mapping, and SCAMPER (Substitute, Combine, Adapt, Modify, Put to another use, Eliminate, Reverse) exercises can stimulate creative problem-solving and generate a diverse pool of potential solutions.

Cost-benefit analyses, risk assessments, and prioritization matrices can aid in objectively comparing and ranking various options, ensuring that selected strategies deliver maximum value while minimizing risks. Collaborative decision-making techniques, such as consensus-building and participatory workshops, enhance buy-in and increase the likelihood of successful implementation.

Final Thoughts

In this chapter, we have delved into the essential aspects of planning quality management for project deliverables. By establishing and implementing a Quality Management Plan (QMP), we've seen how aligning project goals with stakeholder expectations can pave the way for consistent execution. We've discussed the importance of defining specific metrics to assess quality, proactively identifying risks, and involving stakeholders to ensure that quality measures are both realistic and relevant. These steps maintain high standards throughout the project lifecycle and allow for early identification and addressing of potential issues.

Techniques like Lean Six Sigma and regular quality audits ensure that the focus on continuous improvement builds quality into every step of the process. Effective training and regular quality reviews create a culture where high-quality outputs become the norm. By developing clear guidelines, selecting appropriate standards, and fostering open communication and collaboration among team members and stakeholders, projects can achieve superior outcomes. Overall, this chapter underscores that effective quality management is not just about meeting standards, but about creating value and excellence in every aspect of the project.

Reference List

GoLeanSixSigma.com. (2019, April 23). *What is lean six sigma?* GoLeanSixSigma.com. https://goleansixsigma.com/what-is-lean-six-sigma/

Horlick, A. (2024, March 26). *Metrics for Measuring Change Management* . Www.prosci.com. https://www.prosci.com/blog/metrics-for-measuring-change-management

Karpenkova, A. (2023, July 27). *9 Change Management KPIs & Metrics to Track in 2023 | Whatfix* . The Whatfix Blog | Drive Digital Adoption. https://whatfix.com/blog/change-management-kpis/

Laoyan, S. (2023, January 11). *7 Types of Process Improvement Methodologies You Should Know About • Asana* . Asana. https://asana.com/resources/process-improvement-methodologies

Project management lifecycle: Importance and phases . (n.d.). Www.rocketlane.com. https://www.rocketlane.com/resources/psa/project-management-lifecycle

Peterka, P. (2024, May 8). *Focus PDCA: Drive Continuous Improvement & Business Excellence* . SixSigma.us. https://www.6sigma.us/business-process-management-articles/focus-pdca/

Quality management plan . (n.d.). PPM Express. https://ppm.express/glossary/quality-management-plan/

Team, E. (2024, June 14). *What is Quality Control Management in Lean Six Sigma?* SixSigma.us. https://www.6sigma.us/six-sigma-in-focus/what-is-quality-control-management/

Chapter 7 - Human Resource Management

Human Resource Management is all about making the best use of the people in a project. In this chapter, we will explore how defining roles and responsibilities can streamline recruitment and improve team collaboration. Knowing exactly what each person should do enhances accountability and prevents confusion, ensuring that everyone is moving towards the same goals.

The chapter will also delve into creating a comprehensive Human Resource Management plan, which includes strategies for recruitment, training, and performance evaluation. You'll learn how organizational charts and resource calendars can help structure your team and manage their time effectively. By understanding these key aspects, you'll have a better ability to manage your project team and maximize their potential.

Planning Human Resource Management

Identifying Roles and Responsibilities

In any project, clarity concerning roles and responsibilities is crucial for success. Defining what roles are needed streamlines the recruitment and onboarding processes. This understanding helps in assembling a team with the right balance of skills and expertise. Team members knowing their roles minimizes confusion, enhances collaboration, and ensures everyone is working towards common goals.

For instance, let's consider a software development project. You'd need developers, testers, designers, and project managers. Articulating these roles clearly at the project's inception helps in targeting your recruitment efforts effectively. Clear responsibilities reduce overlaps and gaps, promoting efficiency.

The early definition of roles helps establish accountability. When team members understand their specific duties, they are more likely to take ownership of their tasks. This not only propels individual productivity but also fosters a collaborative environment where each member knows who to turn to for specific issues.

Guideline: Create a detailed job description for each role. Outline tasks, required skills, and expected outcomes. This acts as a reference point for both current team members and future recruits.

Human Resource Management Plan

Developing a comprehensive Human Resource Management (HRM) plan is another cornerstone of effective project management. By developing an HRM plan, you can effectively manage the human resources of your project by documenting and consistently following all necessary processes.

An HRM plan typically includes strategies for recruitment, training, and performance evaluation. For example, your recruitment strategy should outline how you will attract the most qualified candidates. Your training strategy should detail how you plan to enhance team members' skills to meet project needs. Lastly, performance evaluation strategies ensure continuous improvement and development.

A well-crafted HRM plan prevents resource conflicts and overlaps by providing a clear roadmap. It helps align human resources with project timelines and goals, making sure the right people are available when needed.

Guideline: Develop an HRM plan template. Include sections for recruitment, training, and performance evaluation, along with a timeline and designated responsibilities.

Organizational Charts

Using organizational charts can significantly improve team structure and communication. These visual aids depict team structure and reporting relationships, simplifying complex hierarchical relationships within the team. They make it easy for everyone to understand who reports to whom, helping to clarify lines of authority and responsibility.

For example, in a large project involving multiple teams, an organizational chart can help team members quickly identify their supervisors and collaborators. This reduces the time spent in figuring out who to contact for specific tasks or approvals, enhancing overall productivity and communication.

Organizational charts help to identify gaps in expertise or personnel. They provide a snapshot of the current team structure, making it easier to spot missing roles or overloaded team members. This allows for timely adjustments, such as hiring new talent or redistributing tasks, to balance the workload.

Guideline: Regularly update the organizational chart. Ensure it reflects any changes in team structure, such as new hires, departures, or role changes. This keeps everyone informed and aligned.

Resource Calendars

Tracking team members' availability is vital for effective project planning and resource allocation. A resource calendar helps by providing a clear view of when team members are available for project tasks. This knowledge aids in timeline planning, guaranteeing that tasks are assigned to the individuals.

For instance, if you are aware in advance that a key developer is scheduled for vacation during a critical phase of the project, you can adjust the project timeline or find a temporary replacement. This proactive approach helps in mitigating risks associated with resource availability.

Resource calendars also enhance accountability. When team members know that their availability is being tracked, they are more likely to adhere to deadlines. This fosters a sense of responsibility and encourages timely completion of tasks.

Guideline: Use software tools to maintain and share resource calendars. Ensure regular updates and accessibility of resource calendars to all team members. This promotes transparency and helps in better resource management.

Conclusion

Effectively planning for a project's human resource requirements is crucial for its success. By identifying roles and responsibilities, developing a structured HRM plan, using organizational charts, and tracking resource availability, you can ensure optimal team structure and efficiency. These strategies not only streamline recruitment and onboarding processes, but also promote collaboration and accountability within the team.

Acquiring Project Team

One of the most critical steps in managing a project team effectively is gaining the right talent. The process of recruitment, selection, negotiation, hiring, and onboarding new team members requires a strategic approach to ensure that the team is well-equipped to meet project goals. Let's delve into how to achieve this.

Recruitment Methods

Recruiting the right candidates starts with understanding and using various methods to attract qualified talent. This involves leveraging multiple channels, such as job boards, social media, company websites, employee referrals, and professional networks. Each channel possesses its strengths and can be customized to target specific candidate pools. For instance, using LinkedIn for recruiting can be effective for sourcing professionals with a solid work history and specialized skills. Current employees can refer to potential hires, pre-vetting them and often resulting in higher retention rates.

Tailoring job descriptions is another crucial element in recruitment. A well-crafted job description should not only detail the required qualifications and responsibilities, but also resonate with the ideal candidates. It should highlight what makes the role unique and appealing, reflecting the company's culture and values. This approach helps in attracting candidates who are not just qualified but also a good cultural fit for the organization.

Selection Process

Once we identify a pool of potential candidates, the next step is to begin the selection process. Establishing clear criteria for choosing the best candidates ensures alignment with project goals and organizational needs. This process typically involves multiple stages, including resume screening, interviews, testing, and evaluations.

Interviews are a fundamental part of the selection process. Structured interviews, where the interviewer asks each candidate the same set of questions, can provide a consistent basis for comparison. Behavioral interviews, which focus on how candidates have handled situations in the past, can offer insights into their problem-solving abilities and work ethic. Testing, whether technical assessments or personality tests, can further validate a candidate's suitability for the role. Evaluations should be thorough, considering both hard skills and soft skills, to ensure a well-rounded assessment of each candidate.

It's essential to involve multiple stakeholders in the selection process to get diverse perspectives. Team members who will work closely with the new hire can provide valuable input on the candidate's cultural fit and potential impact on team dynamics.

Negotiation and Hiring

After selecting the ideal candidate, navigating the offer process is the next critical step. This involves understanding compensation trends to make competitive offers that align with industry standards. Offering a competitive salary and benefits package is essential for attracting top talent and building trust with candidates.

During negotiations, it's important to communicate transparently and honestly about what the company can offer. Flexibility can be a significant advantage; for example, providing options for remote work or additional vacation days can be persuasive factors for many candidates. It's also crucial to address any concerns the candidate may have and find mutually beneficial solutions.

Once an agreement is reached, the HR department starts the formal hiring process. This includes extending a written offer, conducting background checks, and completing all necessary paperwork. Clear communication throughout this phase helps to maintain the candidate's enthusiasm and sets the stage for a positive onboarding experience.

Onboarding Practices

The final step in acquiring suitable team members is integrating them into the organization through effective onboarding practices. A structured onboarding process speeds up the new hire's readiness and familiarizes them with the project's goals and the company's culture. According to research, researchers view onboarding as a comprehensive process rather than a onetime event and suggest that it ideally lasts several months to a year (Maurer, 2024).

On the first day, setting expectations and introducing objectives is critical. New employees need a clear understanding of their job duties and responsibilities from the outset. Social interactions are equally important; arranging welcome lunches or team-building activities can help new hires feel valued and connected to their colleagues.

Effective onboarding also involves providing the tools and resources for new employees to perform their roles efficiently. This includes access to systems and software, training materials, and introductions to key personnel. Regular check-ins during the initial weeks and months can help identify any challenges the new hire may face and provide support as needed.

Creating an online onboarding portal can streamline the process further. Such a portal can house all essential information, training modules, and company policies, making it easily accessible for new employees. Gathering feedback from new hires about their onboarding experience is also beneficial in order to continuously improve the process.

Developing Project Team

Fostering teamwork and enhancing team performance is a vital aspect of human resource management. This section delves into various development techniques that can achieve these objectives. Let's look into four key areas: team-building activities, training and development, performance assessments, and conflict resolution strategies.

Team-Building Activities

Team-building activities are essential for improving collaboration and morale within a team. These initiatives should aim to strengthen interpersonal relationships and foster trust among team members. Here are some effective guidelines for implementing team-building activities:

1. **Choose Activities** : Select activities that cater to your team's interests and dynamics. Options range from outdoor adventures like hiking or obstacle courses to indoor

activities such as problem-solving tasks and collaborative games.

1. **Encourage Participation** : Ensure that all team members are involved. The goal is inclusivity, so pick activities everyone feels comfortable taking part in.

1. **Focus on Collaboration** : Design activities that require team members to work together to solve problems or achieve common goals. For instance, escape rooms and scavenger hunts cause collective effort and strategic thinking.

1. **Schedule Regularly** : Make team-building activities a regular part of your schedule. Regular interactions outside of work settings can help maintain strong relationships and improve team cohesion.

1. **Evaluate Feedback** : After each activity, gather feedback from participants to understand what worked well and what could be improved. This helps in planning future activities more effectively.

Training and Development

Continuous training and development are pivotal for ensuring that team members possess the skills to excel in their roles. These programs not only enhance individual performance but also contribute to overall team innovation and efficiency. Below are some guidelines for effective training and development:

1. **Identify Skill Gaps** : Conduct an assessment to determine the training needs of your team. Understanding these gaps allows you to tailor training programs to address specific requirements.

1. **Offering Tailored Training Sessions:** We customize training sessions to meet the unique needs of your project. Tailored programs are more likely to be relevant and beneficial to team members.

1. **Support Continuous Learning** : Encourage a culture of continuous learning by offering ongoing training opportunities. This can include formal workshops, online courses, or informal knowledge-sharing sessions (Keen, 2023).

1. **Create a Learning Pathway** : Develop a structured learning pathway that outlines the skills and competencies required for career progression. This approach helps team members understand the steps they need to take to achieve their professional goals.

1. **Monitor Progress** : Regularly evaluates the effectiveness of training programs through assessments and feedback. Adjust the content and methods as needed to ensure optimal outcomes.

Performance Assessments

Performance assessments are crucial for gauging team effectiveness and identifying areas for improvement. Regular evaluations provide valuable insights into team strengths and weaknesses, enabling better management decisions. Here are some guidelines for conducting effective performance assessments:

1. **Set Clear Objectives** : Define the criteria and metrics for evaluation before the assessment process begins. Clear objectives align team efforts with organizational goals.

1. **Use a Structured Approach** : Employ a structured approach to performance evaluations. This could involve standardized tools and forms to ensure consistency and fairness in the assessment process.

1. **Conduct regular feedback sessions:** Schedule regular feedback sessions to discuss performance with team members. Constructive feedback helps individuals understand their strengths and areas where they need improvement (Training, 2024).

1. **Involve Peer Reviews** : Incorporate peer reviews into the assessment process. Feedback from colleagues can provide additional perspectives on an individual's performance.

1. **Develop Improvement Plans** : Based on the assessment results, create personalized improvement plans

for team members. These plans should outline specific actions and timelines for achieving performance goals.

Conflict Resolution Strategies

Conflict is an inevitable part of any team dynamic, but effective management of interpersonal tensions is crucial for maintaining a positive team environment. Understanding conflict dynamics and employing proactive conflict resolution strategies can significantly enhance team performance. Here are some guidelines for managing conflicts:

1. **Promote Open Communication** : Encourage open and honest communication among team members. Creating a transparent environment where team members can raise concerns without fear of retribution helps in resolving conflicts early.

1. **Understand Conflict Dynamics** : Take time to understand the underlying causes of conflicts. Recognizing whether the issue stems from personal differences, job roles, or external stressors is important for addressing the root cause.

1. **Employ Mediation Techniques** : Use mediation techniques to facilitate discussions between conflicting parties. A neutral mediator can help navigate the conversation and find common ground.

1. **Provide Conflict Resolution Training** : Equip team members with conflict resolution skills through training programs. Techniques such as active listening, empathy,

and negotiation are essential for handling disputes constructively (Training, 2024).

1. **Establish Clear Policies** : Have clear policies and procedures in place for conflict resolution. Ensure that all team members are aware of these policies and know how to access support when needed.

Managing Project Team

In today's fast-paced project environments, the role of a project manager extends far beyond initial planning and task delegation. One critical ongoing responsibility is overseeing the project team's performance and dynamics. The project manager ensures effective use of resources and efficient achievement of goals through this oversight.

Leadership Styles play a pivotal role in this process. Different leadership approaches impact team performance in various ways. Task-oriented leadership, for instance, focuses on completing specific tasks and is ideal for structured projects with tight deadlines. A people-oriented approach emphasizes building relationships and fostering a supportive environment. Adapting one's style based on team needs can optimize performance and build trust. For example, a new team might benefit from a more directive approach initially, while experienced teams may thrive under a talkative or participative style.

Monitoring Team Performance is another essential duty. By tracking both individual and collective progress, we ensure everyone is aligned with project objectives. Regular check-ins, whether through formal meetings or casual conversations, provide valuable opportunities to address potential issues before they escalate. Metrics, such as Key Performance Indicators (KPIs), provide a quantitative foundation for evaluation. These metrics could include aspects like task completion rates, quality of deliverables, and adherence to timelines.

Effective monitoring requires clear guidelines. Establishing performance benchmarks helps set expectations and provides a reference point for assessing progress. Using project management software can streamline the tracking process by offering real-time updates and detailed reports.

Feedback Mechanisms are crucial for maintaining a healthy and productive team environment. Instituting regular channels for feedback encourages transparency and improves communication. Constructive feedback helps team members understand their strengths and areas for improvement. It also allows managers to make informed decisions about resource allocation and training needs.

Guidelines for providing feedback include being specific, focusing on behaviors rather than personalities, and ensuring it is a two-way street. Encouraging team members to voice their opinions creates an atmosphere of mutual respect and trust. This open dialogue prevents misunderstandings and enhances collaboration.

Recognizing and Rewarding Team Contributions is key to fostering motivation and a culture of success. Acknowledging achievements, no matter how small, boosts morale and encourages continued effort. Recognition can take many forms, from verbal praise and certificates to monetary bonuses and promotions.

Instituting a structured reward system ensures fairness and consistency. Organizations establish a structured reward system to ensure transparency of criteria, making it clear how contributions are measured and valued. Public recognition, such as during team meetings or company newsletters, can also amplify the positive impact.

Incorporating all these elements—leadership styles, performance monitoring, feedback mechanisms, and recognition efforts—into daily project management practices is vital. Not only does it help in keeping the team on track, but it also fosters a supportive and motivating environment where everyone feels valued and empowered to contribute their best.

Final Thoughts

In this chapter, we've explored the essential components of managing a project team and effectively using human resources. From identifying roles and responsibilities to developing a comprehensive Human Resource Management (HRM) plan, we've seen how critical it is to have clear structures in place. Organizational charts and resource calendars further aid in streamlining communication and tracking team availability. These tools not only help in assembling a balanced team, but also ensure that everyone knows their role and is accountable for their tasks.

By focusing on these foundational aspects, you can create a well-organized, efficient, and collaborative project environment. Clear job descriptions and regular updates to organizational charts keep everyone aligned. Using software for resource calendars enhances transparency and accountability. By utilizing this structured approach, you ensure your team is equipped to meet project goals effectively, fostering a productive and harmonious work atmosphere.

Reference List

Biloa, X. S. (2023, October 31). *The Impact of Leadership Style on Employee Job Performance* . Open Journal of Leadership. https://doi.org/10.4236/ojl.2023.124020

Baluch, A., & Main, K. (2022, October 12). *14 onboarding best practices* . Forbes. https://www.forbes.com/advisor/business/onboarding-best-practices/

Effective Human Resource Planning: 6 steps to success | Quixy . (2023, March 24). https://quixy.com/blog/effective-human-resource-planning-6-steps/

Hayes, A. (2023, March 28). *How Human Resource Planning (HRP) Works* . Investopedia. https://

www.investopedia.com/terms/h/human-resource-planning.asp

Keen, D. (2023, August 23). *10 Proven Team-Building Strategies* . Training. https://trainingmag.com/10-proven-team-building-strategies/

Maurer, R. (2024). *New Employee Onboarding Guide-Talent Acquisition* . Www.shrm.org. https://www.shrm.org/topics-tools/news/talent-acquisition/new-employee-onboarding-guide-talent-acquisition

Mazzetti, G., & Schaufeli, W. B. (2022, June 29). *The impact of engaging leadership on employee engagement and team effectiveness: A longitudinal, multi-level study on the mediating role of personal- and team resources* (E. Senel, Ed.). PLOS ONE. https://journals.plos.org/plosone/article?id=10.1371/journal.pone.0269433

Training, A. (2024, July 3). *A Guide to Effective Team Building Strategies in the Workplace* . Aurora Training Advantage; Aurora Training Advantage. https://auroratrainingadvantage.com/articles/effective-team-building-strategies/

Chapter 8 - Communication Management

Managing communication effectively is essential for any project's success. Without clear and consistent communication, misunderstandings can arise, leading to delays and dissatisfaction among stakeholders. This chapter delves into the nuances of crafting communication strategies that ensure every stakeholder is well-informed and engaged. Through understanding each stakeholder's unique needs and preferences, project managers can foster an environment where information flows seamlessly, enabling better decision-making and collaboration.

The chapter will guide you through the process of planning and executing effective communication strategies tailored to various stakeholders. You will learn how to identify stakeholder information needs, ensuring that the right details reach the right people at the right time. We will explore how to define SMART communication objectives that align with broader project goals, helping to keep everyone on the same page. The chapter covers selecting appropriate communication tools and channels to match different information and urgency levels. By the end of this chapter, you will have the tools to create a comprehensive understanding of how to create a robust communication plan and effectively manage it throughout the project lifecycle.

Planning Communications

Planning effective communication strategies is crucial in ensuring that accurate information reaches stakeholders in a timely manner. This section will delve into key elements of planning communication strategies, focusing on identifying stakeholder needs, defining communication objectives, choosing the right tools and channels, and creating a comprehensive communication plan.

Identifying Stakeholder Information Needs
Understanding the unique information needs of different stakeholders is the first step towards effective communication. Each stakeholder group will have varying levels of detail required and preferred frequency for updates. For instance, senior management may need high-level summaries on a bi-weekly basis, while project team members might require detailed daily reports. Assessing these needs upfront helps tailor the communication to ensure relevance and engagement.

To identify stakeholder information needs, begin with a comprehensive stakeholder analysis. This involves listing all potential stakeholders and categorizing them based on their role, influence, and interest in the project. Once identified, engage with each group through surveys, interviews, or meetings to understand their specific requirements. Some questions to consider include:

- What type of information do stakeholders need?

- How often do they prefer to receive updates?

- What format of communication do they find most useful?

By gathering this information early in the project lifecycle, you can prevent unnecessary delays and misunderstandings later on. Stakeholders are more likely to remain engaged if they feel their needs and preferences are being considered from the get-go.

Defining Communication Objectives

With a clear understanding of stakeholder needs, the next step is to define your communication objectives. SMART objectives —Specific, Measurable, Achievable, Relevant, and Time-bound —provide a framework to ensure that communication efforts align with overall project goals and meet stakeholder expectations effectively.

Specific objectives are clear and detailed, providing a precise direction for the communication strategy. For example, "Provide weekly status updates to the project team to keep everyone informed about current progress and upcoming tasks."

Measurable objectives enable tracking progress and assessing the effectiveness of communication. Include criteria, such as the number of updates sent or feedback received, to measure success.

Achievable objectives must be realistic, given the project's scope and resources. Overambitious communication plans can lead to burnout and ineffective information dissemination.

Relevant objectives should align with broader project goals. If the project's success hinges on client satisfaction, prioritize communication objectives that keep clients well-informed and engaged.

Time-bound objectives establish deadlines and frequencies, ensuring regular and timely communication. For example, "Conduct monthly review meetings with stakeholders to discuss project milestones and address any concerns."

Choosing the Right Tools and Channels

Effective communication also depends heavily on selecting the methods and tools. Different tools serve different purposes and preferences; thus, it's important to match the tool to the type of information and urgency.

For formal and detailed communication, emails are usually the best choice. Emails provide a written record and people can easily reference them. Stakeholders can disseminate regular newsletters or detailed project updates via email to keep them well-informed.

Instant messaging platforms like Slack or Microsoft Teams are ideal for quick updates and real-time collaboration. These tools are useful for internal teams needing immediate access to information and quick decision-making.

People can use phone calls or videoconferencing for personalized and sensitive communications, especially when discussing critical issues or seeking immediate feedback.

Meetings can clarify complex points and allow for open dialogue, fostering better understanding and collaboration.

Social media and public announcements can be effective for external stakeholders and broader audiences. Platforms like LinkedIn or company blogs can share significant project milestones and updates, reaching a wider audience efficiently.

Creating a Communication Plan

Documenting your communication strategy in a comprehensive communication plan provides a structured approach to ensure consistency and mitigate risks related to information overload or neglect. A well-crafted communication plan should outline the following components:

1. **Objectives:** Clearly state the SMART objectives you've defined.

2. **Stakeholder Analysis:** Include details from the stakeholder analysis, specifying their information needs and preferred communication channels.

3. **Methods and Tools:** List the chosen methods and tools for each type of communication, along with justifications for their selection.

4. **Frequency and Schedule:** Define the frequency of communication for each stakeholder group and provide a schedule for regular updates or meetings.

5. **Message Content:** Outline the key messages that need to be communicated at different stages of the project. Ensure that messages align with project milestones and stakeholder expectations.

6. **Feedback Mechanisms:** Establish ways for stakeholders to provide feedback. This could include surveys, suggestion boxes, or regular feedback sessions during meetings.

7. **Responsibilities:** Assign roles and responsibilities for communication tasks within the project team. Specify who will draft messages, conducting meetings, and monitoring feedback.

8. **Evaluation and Adjustments:** Establish mechanisms for regularly reviewing and adjusting the communication plan based on feedback and developing project requirements.

Creating a communication plan helps in maintaining consistency across all communication efforts. It ensures that all project stakeholders receive timely and relevant information, mitigating risks related to miscommunication or information gaps. A documented plan serves as a reference guide, aiding new team members or stakeholders in understanding the established communication protocols.

Managing Communications

Executing the communication plan is a critical part of ensuring that project information flows effectively among stakeholders, from the initiation phase to the project's completion. By clearly defining and implementing the planned communication strategies, stakeholders remain aware and involved in the project's progress. This proactive approach minimizes uncertainty and fosters an environment of collaboration.

One key aspect of executing a communication plan is establishing clear guidelines to maintain stakeholder engagement. For instance, regular status updates, whether through weekly meetings, email summaries, or a project management tool, help keep everyone informed about developments, potential risks, and milestones achieved. Using multiple channels ensures that all relevant parties receive the information in a timely manner, catering to their preferences, such as emails for formal updates or instant messaging for quick clarifications.

Encouraging open dialogue among team members is another pivotal element of effective communication. Open communication supports problem-solving and early identification of challenges, which can significantly improve collaborative project success. For example, daily stand-up meetings where team members briefly discuss what they worked on, their plans for the day, and any obstacles they face can foster a transparent work environment. These discussions allow team members to address issues quickly, share insights, and provide support to one another, ultimately leading to a more cohesive team dynamic.

To further facilitate team communication, it is essential to establish norms and practices that encourage sharing and feedback. Team-building activities and workshops can help to create an atmosphere where members feel comfortable voicing their ideas and concerns. Also, using collaborative tools like shared document repositories and project management software can streamline communication and ensure that relevant information is accessible to all.

Managing stakeholder expectations through proactive and transparent communication is crucial, especially during changes or challenges within the project. Regular check-ins with stakeholders can build trust and preserve their confidence. For instance, when encountering a delay because of unforeseen circumstances, informing stakeholders promptly about the new timelines, the reasons for the delay, and the steps being taken to mitigate its impact show accountability and reliability. This transparency not only reassures stakeholders but also engages them in finding solutions and providing support.

In addition, setting realistic expectations from the outset and continuously aligning them with project progress helps manage potential discrepancies between stakeholder assumptions and actual outcomes. One effective practice is to hold kick-off meetings at the beginning of the project, where goals, timelines, and responsibilities are clearly articulated. All parties involved should plan regular meetings to review goals and share updates, ensuring that everyone is well-informed and aligned.

Dealing with communication breakdowns promptly is essential to keeping the project on track. Feedback mechanisms play a vital role in identifying and addressing issues before they escalate. Implementing methods, such as anonymous surveys, suggestion boxes, or regular feedback sessions, allows team members and stakeholders to voice their concerns and suggestions without fear of reprisal. This open line of feedback helps uncover underlying problems that may not be immediately apparent but could hinder project progress if left unaddressed.

For example, if a recurring issue with missed deadlines arises, a feedback session might reveal that the problem stems from unclear task assignments or unrealistic timelines. Addressing these root causes by clarifying roles, adjusting schedules, or providing additional training can prevent future breakdowns and enhance overall team performance.

Learning from past communication breakdowns by conducting post-mortem analyses at the end of significant project phases or after project completion provides valuable insights. These reviews should focus on identifying what went wrong, why it happened, and how to prevent similar issues in the future. Documenting these lessons and integrating them into future communication plans ensures continuous improvement and the avoidance of repeated mistakes.

Effective communication management involves balancing both structured and informal interactions, adapting to the needs of various stakeholders, and being vigilant about potential issues. By embedding these practices into the communication plan and execution, project managers can create a robust framework that supports project success.

Controlling Communications

In today's project management scenario, ensuring effective communication is fundamental to project success. This sub-point addresses how to monitor communication effectiveness and adjust strategies accordingly for optimal information flow.

Monitoring Communication Effectiveness

Effective communication is the lifeblood of any project. To ensure its effectiveness, project managers must employ various tools and approaches. Using feedback loops, such as surveys, can be invaluable in gauging how well communication strategies are working. For instance, after disseminating a new project guideline, a brief survey can help assess whether all stakeholders understood the message clearly and found it useful. Regular feedback collection enables continuous improvement by identifying areas where communication may lack or need change.

Another practical tool is conducting periodic communication audits. These audits involve systematically reviewing all communication channels and content to determine their effectiveness. By analyzing emails, meeting minutes, and internal reports, project managers can find out whether the right messages are reaching the right people at the right time. This process not only highlights strengths but also uncovers weaknesses in the current communication strategy, paving the way for necessary improvements.

Adjusting Communication Plans as Necessary

The dynamic nature of projects often requires adaptability in communication plans. Based on the feedback collected, project managers should regularly review and update these plans. Adaptation ensures that the communication strategy remains relevant and responsive to both stakeholder needs and project developments.

For example, if feedback shows that weekly status meetings are too frequent and cause information overload, we can adjust the frequency to bi-weekly or monthly, depending on project milestones and complexity. In another scenario, stakeholders might express a preference for more visual content, such as infographics or video updates, over lengthy written reports. Incorporating these preferences into the communication plan can significantly enhance engagement and comprehension.

Project changes—such as scope modifications, schedule adjustments, or resource reallocations—cause corresponding updates in communication plans. By aligning communication efforts with the developing project landscape, project managers can ensure that all parties remain informed, engaged, and aligned with project goals.

Maintaining a Central Repository for Project Information

An organized and accessible central repository for project information is integral to effective communication. A centralized database serves as a single source of truth, preventing confusion and fostering accountability among team members. This repository should house all essential documents, including project plans, schedules, meeting minutes, and progress reports.

By having a central hub, team members can easily access the latest information without sifting through emails or disparate file systems. This accessibility is crucial in large projects involving multiple teams or external stakeholders. For instance, a cloud-based collaboration platform like Microsoft SharePoint or Google Drive can serve as an excellent central repository, enabling real-time updates and document sharing. The key is to ensure that the repository is well-organized, with a clear structure and consistent naming conventions for files and folders.

To maintain the repository's effectiveness, regular updates and reviews are necessary. Assigning responsibility for managing the repository to a dedicated team member or administrator can help ensure its ongoing accuracy and reliability. This practice not only enhances transparency, but also aids in tracking project progress and making informed decisions based on up-to-date information.

Reporting on Communication Performance

Transparency is a cornerstone of effective project communication. To foster this transparency, project managers should regularly report on communication performance. These reports can take various forms, such as monthly status updates, quarterly reviews, or end-of-phase summaries. The goal is to provide stakeholders with an overview of communication efforts, highlighting successes, challenges, and planned improvements.

A communication performance report might include metrics, such as response times to stakeholder inquiries, the frequency and attendance of status meetings, and the results of recent feedback surveys. Visual aids like charts and graphs can make these reports more digestible and impactful.

Reporting on communication performance not only keeps stakeholders informed but also encourages their active involvement. When stakeholders see tangible evidence of how communication efforts are contributing to project success, they are more likely to engage proactively and provide valuable input. These reports offer a basis for measuring the impact of any adjustments made to the communication plan, supporting a cycle of continuous improvement.

Conclusion

Effective communication management is pivotal to the success of any project. By monitoring communication effectiveness, project managers can identify areas for improvement and make data-driven decisions. Adapting communication plans based on feedback ensures that strategies remain relevant and engaging. Maintaining a central repository for project information provides a reliable source of truth, fostering clarity and accountability. Last, regular reporting on communication performance promotes transparency and stakeholder involvement.

Communication Methods and Models

Understanding Different Communication Methods

In project management, mastering the various communication methods is pivotal to ensuring effective information dissemination and stakeholder alignment. By recognizing the roles of verbal, non-verbal, and written communication, professionals can enhance clarity and select the most appropriate method for each situation.

People often use verbal communication for immediate interactions, such as meetings or phone calls. It allows for real-time feedback and clarification, which is crucial for urgent matters needing immediate attention. Non-verbal communication, including body language, facial expressions, and gestures, complements verbal communication by enhancing or sometimes contradicting spoken words. For example, a manager's enthusiastic tone paired with positive body language can motivate team members effectively. Written communication is essential for maintaining records and providing detailed instructions. Emails, reports, and memos ensure that all stakeholders have access to consistent and accurate information, reducing misunderstandings.

Incorporating all three methods appropriately ensures that the right message reaches the right audience in the most effective manner. For instance, a combination of written reports and follow-up meetings can effectively communicate complex project updates and address questions.

Exploring Formal vs. Informal Communication

The distinction between formal and informal communication plays a critical role in managing projects efficiently. Formal communication encompasses structured channels, such as official meetings, emails, and reports. This type of communication documents and follows organizational protocols, making it ideal for sharing critical project information, policies, and decisions. For instance, a project kick-off meeting outlining objectives, timelines, and responsibilities is an example of formal communication that sets the stage for the project's success.

Informal communication involves casual interactions among team members, such as impromptu discussions, social gatherings, or quick conversations in hallways or chat applications. These interactions are less structured and help build relationships, foster collaboration, and enhance team cohesion. A simple coffee break conversation can lead to innovative ideas or solutions to project challenges that might not emerge in formal settings.

Balancing formal and informal communication is key to creating a productive work environment. While formal communication ensures accountability and clarity, informal communication promotes a sense of community and openness. Project managers should actively encourage a culture that values and appropriately leverages both types of communication to enhance overall team dynamics.

Using Communication Models

Communication models, like the Shannon-Weaver model, provide valuable insights into the transmission and reception of information. The Shannon-Weaver model comprises several components, including the sender, encoding process, message channel, decoding process, and receiver. Understanding this model helps project managers identify potential barriers to effective communication and develop strategies to overcome them.

For example, noise in the communication channel can distort the message, leading to misunderstandings. This noise could be literal, such as background noise during a conference call, or figurative, such as cultural differences affecting interpretation. By being aware of these potential issues and taking measures, project managers can proactively ensure the accurate reception of the message. They can use clear language, repeat key points, and confirm understanding.

Feedback loops within the Shannon-Weaver model emphasize the significance of two-way communication. Effective communication is not just about sending information, but also about receiving and responding to feedback. Regular check-ins, surveys, and feedback sessions enable project managers to gauge the effectiveness of their communication strategies and make necessary adjustments.

Adapting to Stakeholder Preferences

Tailoring communication approaches based on stakeholder preferences is crucial for fostering successful interactions and minimizing friction. Stakeholders come from diverse backgrounds and have varying expectations, communication styles, and levels of involvement. Adapting your communication strategy to meet these preferences enhances engagement and ensures that everyone remains informed and aligned.

For example, some stakeholders may prefer detailed written reports to fully understand the project's progress, while others might favor brief, verbal updates or visual presentations. Understanding these preferences requires active listening and regular interaction with stakeholders. Building rapport and showing respect for their communication style increases the likelihood of cooperation and support.

Cultural considerations also play a significant role in communication. In international projects, awareness of cultural differences is essential. Direct communication styles popular in Western cultures might clash with more indirect approaches found in Eastern cultures, potentially leading to misunderstandings. Being culturally sensitive and adapting communication styles accordingly shows respect and facilitates smoother interactions.

A guideline for adapting to stakeholder preferences includes:

1. **Identify Stakeholder Preferences:** Conduct surveys or hold one-on-one meetings to understand individual communication preferences.

2. **Categorize Stakeholders:** Group stakeholders with similar preferences together to streamline communication efforts.

3. **Select Channels:** Use the preferred communication channels identified in your stakeholder analysis.

4. **Customize Messages:** Tailor the content and format of messages to suit different audiences.

5. **Seek Feedback:** Regularly ask stakeholders for feedback on communication effectiveness and adjust accordingly.

By following these steps, project managers can create a communication plan that meets the diverse needs of all stakeholders, enhancing collaboration and project success.

Final Thoughts

In summary, this chapter has provided a comprehensive look into effective communication strategies essential for keeping stakeholders well-informed and aligned throughout the project lifecycle. By identifying stakeholder needs and defining clear communication objectives, you ensure that the right information reaches the right people at the right time.

The choice of tools and channels is crucial, as it tailors communication to suit different preferences, and creating a structured communication plan helps maintain consistency and prevent miscommunication.

Equally important is the execution and management of these planned communications. Regular updates, open dialogues, and feedback mechanisms are key to fostering transparency and trust. Adapting your communication plans based on continuous feedback keeps strategies relevant and responsive to changing project dynamics. Maintaining a central repository for project information ensures easy access and clarity for all team members. By implementing these practices, you can build a robust communication framework that supports successful project outcomes and collaborative efforts.

Reference List

9.4 Communication Skills | BABOK® Guide . (2021). Iiba.org. https://www.iiba.org/knowledgehub/business-analysis-body-of-knowledge-babok-guide/9-underlying-competencies/9-4-communication-skills/

Angela. (2024, February 16). *Stakeholder Communication: Benefits, Best Practices, and Management* . Simply Stakeholders. https://simplystakeholders.com/stakeholder-communication/

King, R. (2024, February 16). *5-step stakeholder communication plan* . Finance Alliance. https://www.financealliance.io/stakeholder-communication-plan/

Prasnikar, J. (n.d.). *Fundamental Types of Communication: Verbal, Non-Verbal, Written, Visual* . Optimod.net. https://optimod.net/blog/human-resources-management/fundamental-types-of-communication-verbal-nonverbal-written-visual

PMP 10: Project Communications Management . (2013, March 24). Quizlet. https://quizlet.com/21329134/pmp-10-project-communications-management-flash-cards/

Sivasankari, R. (2020, July 14). *Art of communication in project management* . Pmi.org; Project Management Institute. https://www.pmi.org/learning/library/effective-communication-better-project-management-6480

Włodarczyk, K. (2023, July 21). *The Importance of Stakeholder Communication in Project Management* . Sunscrapers. https://sunscrapers.com/blog/the-importance-of-stakeholder-communication-in-project-management/

Chapter 9 - Risk Management

Managing risks is a vital part of any successful project. The ability to foresee potential issues and plan accordingly can mean the difference between meeting deadlines and going over budget or falling short of objectives. By identifying and evaluating risks early, project managers are better equipped to handle unforeseen challenges, ensuring the project stays on track and within scope.

In this chapter, we dive into the comprehensive approach to risk management. We begin by exploring how to craft a robust risk management plan, emphasizing the importance of involvement from all stakeholders and setting appropriate risk thresholds. You'll learn about various methodologies for identifying risks, such as brainstorming sessions and expert interviews, and see how documentation review plays a crucial role in uncovering recurring threats. We dissect clear roles and responsibilities, budgeting, and timing to show their significance in a successful risk management strategy. Finally, we'll discuss the need for continuous monitoring and effective communication, ensuring that your risk responses remain dynamic and responsive to changing project conditions.

Planning Risk Management

Establishing a comprehensive risk management plan is essential for safeguarding project objectives and ensuring successful completion. This sub-point focuses on creating such a plan, detailing its key components, the role of stakeholder involvement, and the significance of setting risk thresholds and tolerances.

A risk management plan serves as a formalized blueprint for identifying, assessing, and managing risks throughout the project lifecycle. It encourages proactive actions rather than reactive measures, thus mitigating potential issues before they become significant problems. Without a structured plan, teams might overlook critical risks or cannot address them adequately, leading to disruptions that could derail the project. A well-constructed risk management plan lays the foundation for consistent risk handling practices, promoting a culture of continuous vigilance and preparedness.

Creating a robust risk management plan involves several integral components, each playing a crucial role in comprehensive risk mitigation strategies. Let's explore these elements:

1. **Methodologies** : The methodologies chosen dictate how risks are identified, assessed, and managed. These can include qualitative methods like brainstorming sessions, structured interviews, or quantitative approaches, such as probability-impact matrices. The selection of

methodologies ensures thorough coverage and effective risk analysis.

1. **Roles and Responsibilities** : Defining clear roles and responsibilities within the risk management framework is vital. Designating specific individuals or teams to handle different aspects of risk management fosters accountability and clarity. For example, a risk manager may oversee the entire process, while team members focus on specific risks related to their expertise.

1. **Budgeting** : Allocating sufficient resources for risk management activities is essential. This includes funding for risk assessment tools, training programs, and contingency plans. Adequate budgeting ensures that the team has the means to identify, analyze, and respond to risks effectively.

1. **Timing** : Timing outlines when risk management activities will be performed. It is important to integrate risk assessments into regular project reviews and milestones. Early identification of risks allows for prompt mitigation measures, reducing their potential impact on the project.

By incorporating these components, project managers can establish a strong foundation for managing risks, enabling them to choose the most suitable tools and allocate resources efficiently.

Stakeholder involvement is another pivotal element in the risk management process. Engaging stakeholders from various sectors—such as business, government, and NGOs—ensures a wide range of perspectives in risk identification and assessment. According to van Vliet et al. (2020), involving stakeholders significantly widens the scope of risks considered, fostering more comprehensive risk assessments. The project team alone might overlook valuable insights provided by stakeholders. Their active participation promotes agreement for implementing risk management strategies, enhancing collaboration and support throughout the project lifecycle.

Besides stakeholder engagement, establishing clear risk thresholds and tolerances is crucial for prioritizing and managing risks effectively. Risk thresholds are specific points at which risks become unacceptable and require immediate attention. They act as indicators that trigger predefined responses to mitigate potential damage. By setting these thresholds, we prioritize risks based on their impact and probability, ensuring that we allocate resources to address the most critical threats.

Defining risk tolerances involves determining the levels of risk exposure the organization will accept. Factors influencing risk tolerances include organizational objectives, industry standards, stakeholder expectations, and the maturity level of the organization's risk culture. For instance, an organization with a high tolerance for market fluctuations might set higher thresholds for financial risks compared to a more risk-averse entity. By aligning risk tolerances with strategic goals, project managers can make informed decisions that balance risk and opportunity, optimizing resource use for maximum benefit.

Consider the following guidelines when establishing risk thresholds and tolerances:

- **Organizational Objectives** : Align risk thresholds with the overall goals of the organization, considering the desired outcomes and acceptable risk levels.

- **Industry and Regulatory Requirements** : Account for specific industry standards and regulatory guidelines that impact risk management approaches.

- **Stakeholder Expectations** : Understand the risk appetite of key stakeholders, including executives, project sponsors, and clients, to ensure alignment with decision-making.

- **Risk Culture and Maturity** : Assess the organization's risk culture and maturity level, which influence its tolerance for risk and approach to risk management.

For example, a tech company developing innovative software might have a higher tolerance for technical risks because of the inherent uncertainties in the development process. In contrast, a construction firm might have lower tolerances for safety risks because of stringent industry regulations and the potential consequences of accidents.

Evaluating the likelihood and potential impact of risks is essential for setting risk thresholds. High-impact, high-probability risks should receive priority, with lower thresholds triggering more immediate and intensive responses. Implementing early warning systems can help in detecting signs that risks are approaching or exceeding thresholds, enabling timely intervention.

Once risks breach established thresholds, having escalation and response plans in place is critical. These plans outline procedures for elevating risks to higher levels of authority and for detailing steps to mitigate their impact. Regular risk reviews, effective communication protocols, and continuous monitoring ensure that the risk management plan remains dynamic and responsive to changing project conditions.

Identifying Risks

Identifying risks that could affect project objectives is a fundamental aspect of risk management. By employing various methodologies and approaches, project managers can effectively identify potential threats and opportunities. This enables proactive measures and strategic planning to safeguard the project's goals.

Techniques for Risk Identification:

A diverse set of tools and techniques is used to identify risks from different perspectives. One of the most common methods is brainstorming, where team members gather to generate ideas on risks. This collaborative approach encourages open communication and leverages the collective knowledge of the group. By involving individuals with varying expertise and viewpoints, the brainstorming session can uncover risks that might otherwise be overlooked.

Another powerful technique is expert interviews. Interviewing with individuals who have experience in similar projects or industries can provide valuable insights into potential risks. These experts can share lessons learned and highlight areas of concern based on their experiences. The Delphi technique extends this method, where experts provide input anonymously, ensuring unbiased opinions. Iterative rounds of feedback helps achieve a consensus on the most critical risks.

SWOT analysis is another effective tool for risk identification. By examining the project's strengths, weaknesses, opportunities, and threats, a comprehensive picture of potential risks emerges. Strengths and opportunities may highlight areas of positive risk, while weaknesses and threats bring attention to negative risks. This balanced approach ensures that we consider both internal and external factors.

Documentation Review:

Reviewing historical data and documentation from past projects is an invaluable method for identifying risks. Analyzing lessons learned, project archives, and organizational process assets reveals recurring risks and emerging threats. By analyzing lessons learned, project archives, and organizational process assets, we can identify patterns and trends that provide a basis for anticipating future risks.

For instance, if supplier issues have caused delays in previous projects for a company, they should document and review this information when planning new projects. Similarly, reviewing articles and case studies related to industry-specific challenges can expose risks that may not be immediately apparent. By systematically analyzing past performance and outcomes, project managers can proactively address potential issues before they escalate.

Engaging the Team:

Involving the entire project team in the risk identification process fosters a culture of transparency and inclusivity. Every team member brings unique knowledge and perspectives, contributing to a more comprehensive understanding of potential risks. Regular meetings and workshops that focus on risk identification encourage open dialogue and ensure alignment among everyone regarding the project's objectives and potential obstacles.

For example, frontline employees may have a better understanding of operational risks, while senior management might identify strategic risks. By creating an environment where team members feel comfortable sharing their concerns and suggestions, project managers can capture a wide range of risks. Through team engagement, a sense of ownership and accountability is established, motivating everyone to take part actively in risk mitigation efforts.

Risk Register Creation:

Once we identify risks, we must document them systematically. A risk register is a living document that tracks identified risks, their impact, likelihood, and mitigation strategies. This structured approach ensures that all risks are recorded, monitored, and managed throughout the project lifecycle.

The risk register typically includes key details, such as the risk description, potential consequences, assigned risk owner, and proposed mitigation actions. By categorizing risks based on their severity and likelihood, project managers can prioritize their efforts and allocate resources effectively. Regular updates to the risk register ensure it remains relevant and reflect the current state of the project. This dynamic document serves as a central repository for all risk-related information, facilitating informed decision-making and continuous improvement.

Performing Qualitative Risk Analysis

Assessing Risks to Prioritize Them Based on Impact and Likelihood

Effective risk management hinges on the methodical assessment of risks, allowing project managers to prioritize them according to their potential impact and likelihood. This sub-point delineates the key techniques and frameworks essential for assessing and prioritizing risks.

Assessment Techniques

One of the essential techniques for assessing risks is the utilization of probability-impact matrices. These matrices help in visualizing and prioritizing risks based on two primary factors: the likelihood of the risk occurring and its potential impact on the project. For instance, in a probability-impact matrix, you plot risks on a grid where the x-axis represents the likelihood and the y-axis denotes the impact. High-priority risks emerge when both likelihood and impact are significant.

To implement this effectively, start by gathering extensive data from historical records, expert judgments, and stakeholder insights. Collecting data on past projects helps identify patterns and recurring issues that may pose new threats. The probability-impact matrix then translates these qualitative assessments into a visual format, providing an at-a-glance overview that helps in decision-making.

Guideline: Creating a Probability-Impact Matrix

1. Identify all risks.

2. Evaluate the likelihood of each risk.

3. Assess the potential impact of each risk.

4. Plot the risks on the matrix.

5. Review and adjust periodically to reflect changes.

The matrix enables us to identify which risks need immediate attention and which ones we can monitor over time, ensuring a balanced approach to risk management.

Risk Prioritization Frameworks

Different frameworks offer structured approaches to categorize and rank risks by severity. One of the widely used frameworks is the Risk Breakdown Structure (RBS), which organizes risks into hierarchical categories. Each category is further broken down into subcategories, making it easier to pinpoint specific areas of concern. For example, by categorizing risks into financial, operational, regulatory, and technical categories, we can assess and prioritize each risk individually.

Another effective framework is the Failure Mode and Effects Analysis (FMEA). FMEA systematically evaluates possible failures within a process and their consequences, assigning a risk priority number (RPN) to each failure mode. The RPN is a product of the severity, occurrence, and detection ratings, helping to identify which failures require urgent mitigation.

Guideline: Employing FMEA for Risk Assessment

1. List potential failure modes for each process component.

2. Assign ratings for severity, occurrence, and detection for each failure mode.

3. Calculate the RPN by multiplying the three ratings.

4. Rank risks based on their RPN.

5. Develop action plans for high-priority risks to reduce their RPN.

Using multiple frameworks offers a comprehensive understanding of risks, enabling organizations to address the most critical ones first.

Stakeholder Involvement in Assessment

Engaging stakeholders in the risk assessment process is crucial for obtaining accurate insights. Stakeholders bring diverse perspectives, enhancing the comprehensiveness of risk evaluations. In fostering a collaborative environment, team members, sponsors, clients, and end-users actively engage in discussing and evaluating potential risks.

For instance, conducting workshops and brainstorming sessions with stakeholders can unearth hidden risks that might not be immediately apparent through quantitative analysis alone. Such involvement also encourages stakeholders to agree on subsequent risk management strategies, as they perceive their concerns are addressed.

A real-world example could be a construction project where involving the site engineers, safety officers, and contractors in the assessment reveals practical risks related to on-site safety, operational delays, and material quality issues that might otherwise be overlooked. Integrating this feedback ensures a more holistic risk analysis.

Documentation of Analysis Results

Thorough documentation of risk assessment results is vital for tracking progress and improving future risk management efforts. Maintaining detailed records of qualitative analysis, including descriptions of identified risks, their assessed probabilities, affects, and the rationale behind prioritization decisions, provides valuable reference points.

An effective way to document these results is through a Risk Register. This central repository should include comprehensive entries for each risk, covering aspects such as risk owner, assessment dates, mitigation actions, and status updates. Regularly updating the Risk Register enables proactive monitoring and management to develop risks.

Guideline: Maintaining a Comprehensive Risk Register

1. Document each identified risk with a unique identifier.

2. Record the assessed probability and impact.

3. Note the assigned priority level.

4. Detail mitigation strategies and assigned responsibilities.

5. Update the status and review periodically.

For example, a software development project may encounter risks like scope creep or technology changes. By maintaining detailed records, the team can revisit the documented assessments to refine their strategies and avoid similar pitfalls in future projects.

Implementing Risk Responses

Ensuring that your project's objectives are met with minimal disruptions relies on effectively managing project risks. In this section, we'll explore actionable strategies you can implement when responding to identified risks. These strategies aim to minimize their impact and keep the project on track.

Types of Risk Responses

Understanding the risk responses available is critical in crafting an effective risk management plan. The four main types of risk responses, which are avoidance, transfer, mitigation, and acceptance, offer flexibility in dealing with various risks.

Risk Avoidance

Avoiding risks involves changing plans to eliminate the risk altogether. For example, if a new technology poses significant risks because of its untested nature, a project might opt for a more established solution. This avoids the likelihood of unexpected complications. However, avoiding a risk often comes at a higher cost or may require sacrificing possible benefits.

Risk Transfer

Transferring risks shifts the responsibility to a third party. Common methods include insurance policies or contractual agreements where vendors and partners assume certain risks. For instance, purchasing insurance can mitigate financial loss from damages during a project's execution. Alternatively, outsourcing risky project components to a specialized firm can also serve as risk transfer.

Risk Mitigation

Mitigating risks involves taking steps to reduce either the probability of the risk occurring or its impact should it happen. Consider a scenario where budget constraints may threaten project completion. You could mitigate this by negotiating lower prices for materials or reducing the project scope to stay within budget. Mitigation strategies are proactive measures aimed at minimizing potential disruption.

Risk Acceptance

Sometimes the best response is to accept the risk, particularly if it's minor or the cost of mitigation outweighs the benefit. Accepting a low-impact risk, like minor delays, might be more practical than investing resources to eliminate it entirely. Monitoring remains essential even for accepted risks, ensuring they remain within acceptable thresholds and respond promptly to any changes.

Implementation Plans

Once we identify risks and select responses, it is crucial to create clear implementation plans. These plans outline the steps, responsibilities, and timelines for dealing with each risk, ensuring accountability and responsiveness.

Step-by-Step Guidelines

Begin by detailing each action required to address the risk, including specific tasks and milestones. For example, if you're mitigating a supply chain risk, the plan could include identifying alternative suppliers, securing backup inventory, and setting milestone dates for regular status checks.

Assigning Responsibilities

Clearly defined roles ensure everyone knows who handles what. Assigning a risk owner—a person accountable for monitoring and managing the risk—is essential. This role often falls to the team member with the most experience or direct involvement with the risk area.

Timelines

Setting deadlines for each action helps maintain momentum. Make use of Gantt charts or other project management tools to visualize timelines and dependencies. For example, if risk mitigation involves gaining additional funding, the timeline should include stages for proposal writing, submission, approval, and fund disbursement.

Monitoring and Review

Effective risk management doesn't end with implementation; continuous monitoring and review are vital. Regularly assessing both the risks and the effectiveness of your responses allows for adjustments and improvements.

Ongoing Risk Assessment

Consistently evaluate identified risks and remain vigilant for new ones. Use Key Risk Indicators (KRIs) as metrics to measure the probability and consequences of risks. For instance, a sudden increase in supplier lead times may signal an emerging supply chain issue.

Effectiveness Reviews

Periodically review how well your risk responses are working. Are mitigation efforts reducing the likelihood or impact as expected? If not, consider revisiting your strategy.

Conducting these reviews quarterly or after significant project milestones can provide timely insights and opportunities for course correction.

Adaptive Strategies

Be prepared to adapt your strategies based on review findings. Flexibility is the key to risk management. For example, if initial efforts to mitigate a risk prove ineffective, pivot to a risk transfer approach by outsourcing the risky component.

Stakeholder Communication

Communicating with stakeholders about risks and how they're being managed fosters transparency and trust. Open lines of communication ensure that everyone involved stays informed and can contribute valuable perspectives.

Transparency

Being transparent about risks and the potential effects thereof builds credibility. Regularly share updates through meetings, reports, and project management software. Transparency doesn't mean alarming stakeholders, but providing them with a realistic view of the project landscape.

Inclusive Dialogue

Engage stakeholders in discussions about risk responses. Their unique insights can offer alternative strategies or highlight overlooked aspects. For example, involving a finance manager in risk discussions might reveal cost-effective mitigation approaches that the project team hadn't considered.

Feedback Mechanism

Establish a feedback loop for stakeholders to voice concerns and suggestions. Stakeholders can formalize this through surveys, suggestion boxes, or dedicated discussion sessions. Feedback helps refine risk management strategies and ensures they are comprehensive and inclusive.

Final Thoughts

In this chapter, we've explored the critical steps of planning risk management to ensure project success. From developing a thorough risk management plan that includes methodologies, roles, budgeting, and timing, we understand how essential it is to be proactive rather than reactive. Engaging stakeholders and setting risk thresholds and tolerances further enhances our preparedness, allowing us to prioritize and manage risks effectively throughout the project lifecycle.

Identifying risks through techniques like brainstorming, expert interviews, SWOT analysis, and documentation review ensures a comprehensive understanding of potential threats and opportunities. By fostering open dialogue and involving the entire team in the risk identification process, we build a culture of transparency and inclusivity. The creation and maintenance of a dynamic risk register helps track these risks systematically, enabling informed decisions and continuous improvement. This holistic approach to risk management lays the groundwork for successful project completion, safeguarding objectives, and optimizing resource use.

Chatterton, C. (2023, August 17). *The Ultimate Guide to Risk Prioritization* . Hyperproof. https://hyperproof.io/resource/the-ultimate-guide-to-risk-prioritization/

GreyCampus. (2000). *Risk Identification tools and techniques | Certified Associate In Project Management* . Greycampus.com. https://www.greycampus.com/opencampus/certified-associate-in-project-management/risk-identification-tools-and-techniques-in-capm

How to Identify Project Risks in Project Management? (2024, March 28). Knowledgehut.com. https://www.knowledgehut.com/blog/project-management/project-risk-identification

Sokolov, D. (2022, March 28). *PMO Risk Management Best Practices* . PPM Express. https://ppm.express/blog/pmo-risk-management-best-practices/

Team, E. (2024, July 23). *COVID-19 Situation: Six Sigma Ongoing Training Announcements* . SixSigma.us. https://www.6sigma.us/six-sigma-in-focus/risk-prioritization-matrix/

Twproject . (2019, June 13). *Twproject: project management software* . Twproject: Project Management Software, Bug Tracking, Time Tracking, Planning. https://

twproject.com/blog/risk-response-strategies-mitigation-transfer-avoidance-acceptance/

Wojno, R. (2022, August 13). *The importance of risk mitigation* . Monday.com Blog. https://monday.com/blog/project-management/risk-mitigation/

van Vliet, O., Hanger-Kopp, S., Nikas, A., Spijker, E., Carlsen, H., Doukas, H., & Lieu, J. (2020, June 1). *The importance of stakeholders in scoping risk assessments—Lessons from low-carbon transitions* . Environmental Innovation and Societal Transitions. https://doi.org/10.1016/j.eist.2020.04.001

Chapter 10 - Procurement Management

Procurement management is the art of obtaining the goods and services a project needs to succeed. It encompasses everything from identifying what those needs are, to deciding how and when to gain them, and finally ensuring that every resource aligns with the project's goals. By effectively managing procurement, project managers can ensure they secure all necessary components in a timely and cost-effective manner, contributing significantly to the success of the project.

In this chapter, we will delve into the various facets of procurement management, starting with planning procurement strategies. You will learn how to identify and evaluate your project's needs, develop a comprehensive procurement management plan, and select the best suppliers through thorough research and evaluation. We will also explore conducting procurements by engaging vendors using well-defined Requests For Proposals (RFPs), systematic bid assessments, and effective negotiation techniques. Finally, we will look at controlling procurements through continuous vendor performance monitoring and handling contract modifications, followed by closing procurements with proper verification, administrative closure, audits, and capturing lessons learned. Each step is crucial for ensuring that projects run smoothly, on time, and within budget.

Planning Procurement

Determining what to procure, how to procure, and when to procure are fundamental steps in developing an effective procurement strategy. To begin with, identifying the goods and services required for project completion is essential. This requires conducting a detailed analysis of the project's objectives to ensure that all necessary resources are secured. Aligning these needs with project goals ensures that procurement efforts directly contribute to the overall success of the project.

For instance, if a project aims to develop new software, identifying the hardware, software licenses, and skilled personnel will be crucial. This step ensures that the project does not overlook any critical resources, which could otherwise cause delays or increased costs. Understanding the exact specifications of what needs to be bought helps in making informed decisions, improving efficiency, and reducing the risk of acquiring non-essential items.

Once we identify the needs, the next step is to create a comprehensive procurement management plan. This plan should detail the procurement processes and approaches, ensuring that all activities adhere to timelines and resource availability. A well-structured plan serves as a roadmap, guiding the procurement team through each stage of the process. It includes defining procurement methods, setting budgets, establishing timelines, and outlining roles and responsibilities.

To develop this plan, project stakeholders need to collaborate to ensure alignment with the procurement strategies. Incorporating their inputs helps to create a more robust and realistic plan. For instance, when we engage the finance department, they can aid in budget planning, and when we consult with technical teams, we can ensure that we accurately capture the specifications and requirements. The plan serves as a living document we can adjust as needed, providing flexibility to respond to changes in the project environment.

Selecting the right suppliers or service providers is equally important in procurement management. This step involves thorough research and evaluation to optimize both quality and cost. By evaluating potential suppliers based on criteria such as pricing, quality, reliability, and service delivery, we ensure we choose the best fit. It is important to go beyond just considering costs.

One practical approach is to create a vendor shortlist followed by a detailed assessment process. This process might include sending out Requests for Proposals (RFPs) to gather detailed information about potential suppliers. Comparing these proposals against predefined criteria helps in making objective and informed decisions. Establishing long-term relationships with trusted suppliers can lead to better negotiation terms and more reliable service, ultimately benefiting the project.

An essential aspect of selecting suppliers is conducting a site visit or requesting samples where possible. This hands-on approach provides deeper insights into the supplier's capabilities and reliability. Engaging in direct communication with potential suppliers also offers an opportunity to clarify any uncertainties and build rapport, laying the foundation for a collaborative partnership.

Evaluating risks associated with procurement activities is another critical component. Procurement often involves various risks, such as supply chain disruptions, price fluctuations, and quality issues. Implementing proactive planning and mitigation strategies is vital for uninterrupted project progress. Project teams can develop contingency plans that can be activated if needed by identifying potential risks early.

For example, if a particular supplier has occasional delays, having a backup supplier than part of the contingency plan can mitigate this risk. Regularly reviewing and updating the risk management plan ensures it remains relevant and effective. Building strong relationships with suppliers and maintaining open lines of communication can also help in identifying and addressing risks promptly.

Incorporating risk assessment results into the procurement management plan can enhance the plan's effectiveness. This integration ensures that risk management measures are not an afterthought but an integral part of the procurement strategy. Periodic reviews and audits of procurement activities help in identifying any deviations from the plan and taking corrective actions as needed.

Conducting Procurements

Engaging vendors to submit proposals through well-defined Requests for Proposals (RFPs) is paramount in procurement management. A well-crafted RFP can enhance the quality of responses and foster competitive pricing, ultimately leading to better procurement outcomes. The RFP should be clear and comprehensive, detailing the requirements, expectations, and evaluation criteria. This transparency ensures vendors understand what is required and can tailor their proposals accordingly.

The first step in creating an effective RFP involves defining the project scope. Categorizing elements into must-have, nice-to-have, and not needed is essential. This categorization will help in formulating precise questions that guide the vendors on what is critically important. Close-ended questions for must-have elements simplify objective evaluations. To ensure a holistic approach to vendor assessments, the RFP should distribute these elements across different sections.

Once the RFP is issued, the next crucial phase involves systematically assessing bids based on predefined criteria. This stage involves establishing RFP priorities, where it's vital to communicate the importance of various factors clearly. Often, capabilities and experience weigh more than price. Transparency about these priorities in the RFP encourages vendors to provide relevant and interesting responses. Establishing scoring criteria helps maintain objectivity during evaluations. Developing a guide for stakeholders involved in scoring can eliminate ambiguity and ensure consistency in how they assess proposals.

Internal stakeholder engagement is equally important. Individual stakeholders affected by the procurement outcome should have a say in evaluating vendor proposals. Engaging them individually rather than in large groups prevents dominant opinions from skewing the assessment and ensures a balanced evaluation. This approach is especially important when dealing with complex procurements requiring input from various departments or experts, such as IT and HR teams.

Discrepancies in scores among evaluators are normal but need addressing to ensure fairness and clarity in the evaluation process. By understanding and resolving these differences, we can uncover whether certain questions were misinterpreted or require rephrasing for future RFPs. Regularly discussing and reviewing scores among evaluators can improve the overall assessment process.

Engaging in dialogue to arrive at mutually beneficial agreements during contract negotiations is another critical aspect of procurement management. Effective negotiation aims to achieve terms that benefit both parties and lay the groundwork for long-term partnerships. Open communication and flexibility are key here. Both parties should have confidence that they understand and respect each other's needs and constraints. By documenting negotiations, both parties can prevent misunderstandings and have a reference for future interactions.

Successful negotiation often leads to better contract terms, including clear deliverables, timelines, and payment schedules. It's essential to balance firmness and flexibility to reach the most helpful agreement. This process builds trust and establishes a strong foundation for the working relationship, potentially leading to continued collaboration beyond the initial contract.

Completing the procurement process by executing well-structured contracts with selected vendors is the final step. These contracts should clearly outline expectations and obligations for both parties. A well-drafted contract includes detailed descriptions of goods or services, delivery schedules, performance metrics, and payment terms. Clarity in contracts helps in managing expectations and reduces the risk of disputes.

To execute contracts, it is crucial to ensure that all legal and regulatory requirements are met. It's crucial to involve legal experts in drafting and reviewing contracts to safeguard against potential legal challenges. Proper documentation throughout this process is vital for compliance and serves as a record for future reference.

Once the contract is in place, ongoing management is necessary to ensure adherence to its terms. Regular reviews and performance assessments keep vendors accountable and can highlight areas needing improvement. To ensure smooth execution of the contract, it is important to maintain transparent communication channels to address any issues promptly.

Apart from the main steps, there are a few effective approaches to strengthen the procurement process. Developing a thorough understanding of market dynamics and supplier capabilities can inform better decision-making. Leveraging technology, such as procurement software, can streamline processes and improve efficiency. Automated systems for tracking and evaluating bids, managing contracts, and monitoring vendor performance can save time and reduce errors.

Building strong relationships with vendors through fair and transparent dealings fosters mutual respect and can lead to better collaboration. Suppliers who feel valued and treated fairly are more likely to go above and beyond in delivering high-quality goods and services. Regular meetings, feedback sessions, and joint problem-solving initiatives can strengthen these relationships.

Another important aspect is risk management in procurement. Identifying potential risks early in the process and developing strategies to mitigate them can prevent disruptions. This includes assessing the financial stability of suppliers, ensuring compliance with regulations, and maintaining alternative sources of supply.

Last, continuous improvement is essential for effective procurement management. Capturing lessons learned from each procurement cycle and integrating them into future processes can enhance efficiency and outcomes. Regularly updating procurement policies and procedures to reflect industry best practices and technological advancements ensures that the procurement function remains agile and responsive to changing needs.

Controlling Procurements

Monitoring vendor performance and ensuring contract compliance are vital components in procurement management that significantly contribute to project success. Effective techniques for overseeing these areas can lead to more accountable practices, better quality deliverables, and stronger vendor relationships.

Regular assessments of vendor performance are crucial for promoting accountability and maintaining high standards. By consistently evaluating how vendors perform against contract specifications, organizations can pinpoint areas needing improvement and commend those meeting expectations. Implementing a scorecard system that quantitatively measures various performance aspects, such as quality, delivery time, cost-effectiveness, and responsiveness, can be beneficial (Order.co, 2024). Regular performance reviews might involve periodic site visits, customer feedback collection, and analysis of performance data. These evaluations not only ensure adherence to agreed-upon terms but also foster a culture of continuous improvement among vendors.

Another critical aspect is handling modifications to contract terms in a controlled manner. Contract changes are sometimes necessary due to developing project requirements or unforeseen circumstances. However, without a formal change management process, these modifications can lead to confusion and disputes. A robust change management process should involve all necessary stakeholders from both the organization and the vendor side. Establishing clear procedures for requesting, approving, and documenting contract changes ensures everyone agrees. This might include defining who has the authority to request changes, setting timelines for reviewing and implementing changes, and maintaining detailed records of all modifications and their justifications.

Verifying compliance with contractual obligations is another key practice in effective procurement management. Regular compliance checks help ensure that all parties fulfill their duties as stipulated in the contract. Conducting these reviews can enhance project governance and mitigate risks by identifying potential issues early and addressing them promptly. Compliance checks may involve reviewing deliverables against contract requirements, monitoring timelines, and verifying that payment terms are met. For instance, if a vendor's delivery consistently falls short in quantity or quality, immediate discussions and corrective actions are necessary to prevent cascading project delays or failures (Barnes, 2023).

Maintaining thorough records of procurement-related activities is essential for fostering transparency and accountability. Detailed documentation provides a reference point for lessons learned and best practices, which can be invaluable for future projects. Effective record-keeping involves cataloging every aspect of the procurement process, from initial vendor selection and contract negotiations to performance evaluations and compliance reviews. These records should be readily accessible and well-organized to facilitate audits, support decision-making, and ensure compliance with legal and regulatory requirements. Robust documentation can aid in resolving disputes by providing a clear paper trail of agreements, communications, and actions taken.

Closing Procurements

The final steps of the procurement process require ensuring that all aspects are properly concluded and documenting lessons learned for future projects. This phase, known as completion and closeout, includes important actions to confirm vendor accountability, complete administrative tasks, conduct audits, and gather insights.

First, verify delivery of contracted goods or services. This step ensures that vendors have fulfilled their obligations as per the contract terms. To confirm procurement completion, it is necessary to inspect and test the deliverables according to the agreed-upon standards. For instance, if the project involved procuring software, conducting acceptance tests will ensure that the software meets the required specifications and performs as expected. To maintain accountability, promptly address any deviations or issues with the vendor. This verification process not only validates that we have met the project goals, but also helps us build trust with reliable suppliers for future endeavors.

Next, completing all administrative tasks related to procurement contracts is vital for a smooth closure. This includes timely closure of contracts and completing payments to clear financial obligations. Using a contract closeout checklist is one effective method to ensure nothing is overlooked. This checklist can include tasks such as confirming the submission and payment of all invoices, receiving and analyzing testing reports, and ensuring the return of government-furnished property. Administrative closure also involves collecting any warranties or other final deliverables from the vendor. Timely execution of these tasks prevents any lingering issues that could arise later and provides a clean break point for both the buyer and the seller.

Conducting procurement audits is another critical step in this phase. These audits review the entire procurement process, from solicitation to contract fulfillment, to identify areas for improvement. By examining contract documentation, supplier performance records, and compliance with procurement policies, organizations can pinpoint inefficiencies and develop strategies for better practices in future projects. For example, if a project faced delays because of extended negotiation periods, an audit might reveal the need for clearer guidelines or more streamlined processes. Audits contribute significantly to ongoing professional development by highlighting both successes and shortcomings, offering a comprehensive view of what worked well and what didn't.

Finally, capturing insights gained during the procurement process fosters a culture of continuous improvement. By documenting lessons learned, we can share valuable knowledge with team members and stakeholders, ensuring that we don't repeat the same mistakes and reinforce good practices. A structured approach to documenting lessons learned may involve organizing debriefing sessions, where all key participants discuss their experiences and provide feedback. These discussions can uncover various learning points, such as effective communication channels or the importance of early stakeholder engagement. By compiling these insights into a report, organizations create a reference guide that can inform future procurement activities and enhance overall project management capabilities.

Summary and Reflections

In this chapter, we explored the essential steps of procurement management. We began by identifying what needs to be procured and how to align these requirements with project goals. We emphasized the importance of creating a detailed procurement management plan, incorporating input from all stakeholders to ensure a robust strategy. The discussion also emphasized the importance of thoroughly evaluating suppliers to select the right ones, highlighting the need for quality and reliability. The stakeholders underscored the importance of effective risk management strategies to handle potential disruptions and maintain project momentum.

We then delved into the process of conducting procurements, from crafting clear and comprehensive RFPs to systematically assessing vendor bids. The chapter outlined best practices for engaging internal stakeholders and ensuring balanced evaluations. The chapter emphasized the importance of successfully negotiating contracts and setting clear expectations for long-term supplier relationships. Finally, we covered controlling procurements through regular performance reviews, managing contract modifications, and ensuring compliance. These steps help to achieve project success and establishing effective procurement practices.

Reference List

6 Phases of Project Procurement Management Process Flow . (n.d.). Visure Solutions. https://visuresolutions.com/tender-and-procurement-guide/phases-of-procurement-management-process/

6.1 Completion & Closeout . (n.d.). Spo.hawaii.gov. https://spo.hawaii.gov/procurement-wizard/manual/completion-closeout/

Barnes, D. (2023). *What is Vendor and Contract Lifecycle Management (VCLM)?* Gatekeeperhq.com. https://

www.gatekeeperhq.com/blog/vendor-and-contract-lifecycle-management-vclm

Order.co . (2024, August 19). Order.co. https://www.order.co/blog/vendor-management/vendor-management-lifecycle/

Procurement Strategy: 8 Essential Steps to Success - Procurify . (2016, February 25). Www.procurify.com. https://www.procurify.com/blog/procurement-strategy-in-8-steps/

ProcureAbility. (2021, April 28). Procurement Process 101: The Stages of Procurement . ProcureAbility. https://procureability.com/what-are-the-stages-of-procurement-process/

Symms, R. D. (2021, January 14). A guide to RFP evaluation criteria: Basics, tips and examples . Responsive. https://www.responsive.io/blog/rfp-evaluation-criteria/

The Essential Guide to Understanding the RFP Process . (n.d.). Vendorful. https://vendorful.com/rfp-process/

Conclusion

As we reach the end of this guide, let's take a moment to reflect on the journey we've undertaken together. We've delved into many facets of program management, unraveling its complexities and transforming them into manageable, understandable segments. Whether you are a busy professional preparing for the PMP exam, a mid-level manager looking to augment your project management skills, or someone transitioning into a new role in program management, the knowledge gained through these pages is both practical and empowering.

At the core of program management lies the intricate balance of aligning multiple projects towards broader organizational objectives. Understanding this foundational principle is crucial for any aspiring program manager. Rather than focusing solely on individual projects, a program manager's vision spans across various interconnected projects, ensuring they collectively contribute to the strategic goals of the organization. This holistic approach not only optimizes resources but also drives significant value and achieves sustained success.

In real-world settings, the concepts discussed throughout this book become invaluable tools in your professional toolkit. Picture yourself stepping into the role of a program manager. One day, you'll face leading a diverse team, each member working on different projects that ultimately converge on the same strategic endpoint. Picture using strategies to expect potential problems and taking action to prevent them from becoming major hurdles. By doing so, you mitigate risks, foster a productive environment, and lead your team towards successful project completions. By demonstrating this skill alone, you can set yourself apart as a leader who is prepared, insightful, and capable of steering projects through uncertain waters with confidence.

Beyond risk management, consider the importance of stakeholder engagement. Effective communication and relationship-building with stakeholders can dramatically influence the outcome of your projects. When stakeholders feel heard and valued, their support can prove instrumental in overcoming hurdles and driving projects forward. Applying these principles in your daily routine will not only enhance your effectiveness as a program manager but also strengthen your professional relationships, paving the way for further career advancements.

This book has also underscored the necessity of flexibility and adaptability. The dynamic nature of program management means that change is often the only constant. Embracing change, rather than resisting it, enables you to pivot swiftly and make informed decisions that align with developing circumstances. For example, an unexpected shift in market conditions might cause a realignment of project priorities. Your ability to identify such shifts and adapt your strategies accordingly ensures that your projects remain relevant and impactful.

As you prepare for the PMP exam, let this guide serve as a testament to your hard work and dedication. We have meticulously covered essential concepts, from initiation and planning to execution, monitoring, and closing. We have crafted each chapter to build your confidence and competence, providing you with a robust framework to tackle the exam questions head-on. Remember, the knowledge you possess now is ample and well-rounded, equipping you to navigate the complexities of the exam with poise.

Yet, despite the comprehensive nature of this guide, the journey of learning does not end here. Program management is a field characterized by continuous evolution, driven by technological advancements, emerging trends, and innovative practices. Therefore, it is vital to maintain an attitude of perpetual learning. Subscribe to industry publications, take part in workshops, and engage in webinars. These activities will keep you abreast of the latest developments, enriching your expertise and keeping your skills sharp.

Networking with other professionals in the field can offer fresh perspectives and insights. Engage in discussions, attend conferences, and seek mentorship opportunities. Sharing experiences with fellow program managers can uncover new strategies, reveal best practices, and broaden your understanding of various approaches to common challenges. These connections often prove to be invaluable sources of knowledge and support throughout your career.

Opportunities for growth and improvement are present along the path to becoming an excellent program manager. Embracing this mindset will not only keep you competitive, but also inspire others around you. As you ascend in your career, you become a beacon of knowledge and a source of inspiration for upcoming program managers. Your commitment to learning and excellence sets a standard within the industry, fostering a culture of continuous development and innovation.

Finally, as you gear up for the PMP exam, take a moment to acknowledge the effort you have invested in reaching this point. The concepts you have mastered, the practical applications you have envisioned, and the continual learning you have embraced all culminate in a solid foundation of program management prowess. Approach the exam not merely as a test, but as an opportunity to showcase your understanding and capabilities. Confidence stems from preparation, and you are thoroughly prepared.

Embrace the challenge with assurance and let your knowledge shine. Trust in your abilities and keep in mind that you have the tools not just to pass the exam, but to excel as a program manager. Your future is promising, filled with potential achievements and professional fulfillment. And whenever you need a reminder of your capabilities, revisit these pages and reaffirm your grasp of the concepts that will drive your success.

Thank you for allowing this guide to be part of your journey. The dedication you have shown is commendable, and I know you will achieve great things in your program management career. Congratulations on how far you've come, and best of luck on the road ahead!

Made in the USA
Las Vegas, NV
19 September 2024

95494823R10105